A LEGACY OF BLESSINGS

for Generations to Come

Dr. D. Robert Kennedy

World rights reserved. This book or any portion thereof may not be copied or reproduced in any form or manner whatever, except as provided by law, without the written permission of the publisher, except by a reviewer who may quote brief passages in a review.

The author assumes full responsibility for the accuracy of all facts and quotations as cited in this book. The opinions expressed in this book are the author's personal views and interpretations, and do not necessarily reflect those of the publisher.

This book is provided with the understanding that the publisher is not engaged in giving spiritual, legal, medical, or other professional advice. If authoritative advice is needed, the reader should seek the counsel of a competent professional.

Copyright © 2022 Dr. D. Robert Kennedy
Copyright © 2022 TEACH Services, Inc.
ISBN-13: 978-1-4796-1431-8 (Paperback)
ISBN-13: 978-1-4796-1432-5 (ePub)
Library of Congress Control Number: 2021923254

Unless otherwise indicated, all Scripture quotations are taken from the New King James Version®, copyright © 1982 by Thomas Nelson.

Scripture quotations marked ESV are taken from the Bible (The Holy Bible, English Standard Version®), copyright © 2001 by Crossway Bibles, a publishing ministry of Good News Publishers. ESV Text Edition: 2016.

Scripture quotations marked NIV are taken from the Holy Bible, New International Version®, NIV®, copyright ©1973, 1978, 1984, 2011 by Biblical, Inc.™)

Scripture quotations marked ASV are taken from The American Standard Version, published in 1901 by Thomas Nelson & Sons.

Scripture quotations marked with the designation "GW" are taken from GOD'S WORD®. © 1995, 2003, 2013, 2014, 2019, 2020 by God's Word to the Nations Mission Society. Used by permission.

Scripture quotations marked HCSB are taken from the Holman Christian Standard Bible®, copyright © 1999, 2000, 2002, 2003, 2009 by Holman Bible Publishers. Used by permission. Holman Christian Standard Bible®, Holman CSB®, and HCSB® are federally registered trademarks of Holman Bible Publishers.

Scripture quotations marked MSG are taken from THE MESSAGE, copyright © 1993, 2002, 2018 by Eugene H. Peterson. Used by permission of NavPress. All rights reserved. Represented by Tyndale House Publishers, Inc.

Scripture quotations marked NASB are taken from the New American Standard Bible, copyright © 1960, 1962, 1963, 1968, 1971, 1972, 1973, 1975, 1977, 1995 by The Lockman Foundation, La Habra, Calif. All rights reserved.

Scripture quotations marked NIRV are taken from the New International Reader's Version, copyright © 1995, 1996, 1998, 2014 by Biblica, Inc.®. Used by permission. All rights reserved worldwide.

Scripture quotations marked NLT are taken from the Holy Bible, New Living Translation, copyright © 1996, 2004, 2015 by Tyndale House Foundation. Used by permission of Tyndale House Publishers, Inc., Carol Stream, Illinois 60188. All rights reserved.

Scripture quotations marked NRSV are taken from the New Revised Standard Version Bible, copyright © 1989 National Council of the Churches of Christ in the United States of America. Used by permission. All rights reserved worldwide.

Scripture quotations marked TLV are taken from the Tree of Life Translation of the Bible, copyright © 2015 by The Messianic Jewish Family Bible Society.

Published by

www.TEACHServices.com • (800) 367-1844

Dedication

This collection is dedicated to Mrs. Zenobia Davis ("Aunt Zen"), one of the great women to have poured blessings into my life. When I was 14 years of age, Aunt Zen heard me singing bass in a little country church choir. She said she was so impressed about my voice that she said to the woman sitting beside her, "I want that young man to sing in my college choir." I did attend the college but did not get to sing in her choir because of my work schedule. Even though I did not sing in her choir, Aunt Zen nurtured me in various ways. When she discovered that I was interested in a certain young lady on campus, she wisely said, "That young lady [she gave her name] would be good for you." Until this day, she has never told me what she meant. However, when I proposed to marry "that young lady," Aunt Zen helped to plan and direct the wedding. My wife and I have been married for 50 years plus now and feel blessed to call Aunt Zen our mother and friend. She is the godmother of Robert, III, our first son, and still serves as an inspiration for our lives. At a year short of 100, Aunt Zen is very sharp mentally. In dedicating this book to her, I feel blessed to have her in my life, and I want her to know how much I am still appreciative of her blessing on me. In my young teens, she saw potential in me, and, through the years, I have fondly thought of her as having been one of the powerful influences in the realization of my dreams. Thanks, Aunt Zen. You have blessed me, and that is one reason why I rejoice that I have the privilege to bless you.

When we talk about the ripple effect of blessings, among other things, we are talking about the blessings that are passed from one generation to another. A first blessing has mighty possibilities.

Yet, it is a great tragedy when it can be said, God gave them the blessings, but "the blessings they received brought no blessing to the world" (Ellen G. White, *Acts of the Apostles*, p. 14).

Contents

Foreword...9

1. The Genesis of Blessings........................15
2. The Legacy of Blessings........................21
3. The Blessings of Marriage......................27
4. The Blessings of Children......................35
5. The Blessings of Family........................41
6. The Blessings of Sabbath Rest..................49
7. The Blessings of Work..........................55
8. The Blessings of Daily Provisions..............63
9. The Blessings of Obedience.....................71
10. The Blessings of Salvation....................79
11. The Blessings Redirected.....................85
12. The Blessings on Noah........................91
13. The Blessings of Abraham.....................97
14. The Blessings from Melchizedek..............103

15. The Blessings of Tithing 109

16. The Blessings of Aging 115

17. The Blessings of Mercy 121

18. The Blessings of Godly Relationships 127

19. She Will Be a Blessing to You 133

20. Passing on the Blessings 139

21. Don't Throw Away Your Blessings 143

22. The Blessings of Peacemaking 149

23. God Bless You My Son 155

24. Resented for Being Blessed 161

25. The Blessing of Being in God's Presence 165

26. Blessings for Barren Women 171

27. Wrestling for a Blessing. 177

28. A Name Change for a Blessing 183

29. A Blessed Destiny 189

30. Generational Blessings 193

31. The Blessings of Dreaming. 199

Contents

32. The Blessings of Self-Control...................205

33. The Blessings of Integrity.....................209

34. The Blessings of Positive Living..............215

35. The Blessings of a Godly Character...........221

36. The Blessings of Truthfulness.................227

37. The Blessings of Principled Living............231

38. The Blessings of Resiliency...................235

39. The Blessings of Forgiveness 241

40. The Blessings of Discernment 247

41. The Blessings on Joseph......................251

42. Blessed to Bless Others......................255

43. Blessings from a Deathbed....................259

44. Finding a Blessed Place of Rest..............263

45. The Blessings We Leave Behind 269

46. Blessing the Lord............................275

Reflections on A Legacy of Blessings...............281

Foreword

In the preface to the Constitution of the United States of America (1787), there are a few words that some people might be tempted to pass over while giving attention to others. Yet, these frequently overlooked words are profoundly important. Here are the words: "… secure the Blessings of Liberty to ourselves and our Posterity." One could say that these words are an echo of the blessing in Genesis in which God said to Abraham: "I will make of you a great nation; I will bless you and make your name great; and you shall be a blessing. I will bless those who bless you, and I will curse him who curses you; and in you all the families of the earth shall be blessed" (Gen. 12:1–3, NKJV).

The phrasing and parsing of the words in the Constitution, as I have quoted them here, are true reminders of the covenant blessings to Abraham and his progeny. Such blessings have been passed even to our generation. According to biblical understanding, to share in the blessings we need to have faith and live in true obedience to God (Gal. 3:14). But once we receive the blessings, they are not ours to keep; they are ours to pass on to the generations to come (see Ps. 145:4).

As I undertake the task of writing this foreword, I think of the wonderful blessings of my life and the influence of my parents, siblings, husband, children, friends, and church community—all together forming a unitive ring of a family. Together we have been able to pass on our legacy of blessings to generations. According to the legacy project.org, legacy is really about life and living. It helps a person to determine the kind of life he or she wants to live and share. This is why I center on my family because I consider that the unity we share is a most profound blessing that is not shared by many families today. I am not desiring to boast, but I am giving God praise for how my family has been able to maintain the intensity of relationship we share. Our father—Robert Nathaniel Kennedy—used to say, "You can do good, or you can do well. But doing good is better than doing well." When we asked him what he meant, he would say, "It is not how much we have or how successful we are but whether we are blessed with a family unity to share with others."

Dad's father died when he was twelve years old, and Mom's mother died when Mom was sixteen years old. Thus, both of our parents grew into their late teens with only one parent. But Dad and Mom made early pledges to claim God's blessings and to share such blessings with their family and community. After committing their lives to Christ in their early twenties, they got married and decided that they would rear the kind of family that would stay under the panoply of the divine blessings. Together Dad and Mom were blessed to have ten children. And although some of the children went away from home in their early teens, yet it is a marvel that all ten children are leaders and ordained elders of churches in the varied places in which they have lived.

When asked the secret of why each child has been so effective in leadership, each child credits Dad and Mom for having built up the family. They began and closed each day at the family altar with worship and had a consistent time of prayer in the wee hours of the morning. As they would tell us later, when we asked what they were doing in always talking so loudly from their bedroom so early in the mornings, they would say, "We were praying for each child by name." As we grew and revisited the old homestead where we grew up, many of the neighbors who joined our family church would say to us, "We want to thank your parents for the early morning worships that we heard from your house." When Dad and Mom went to live in Canada, which became their home for thirty years, we heard similar comments of the positive influence that they cast upon their neighbors. They were spoken of as an exemplary couple in their church and community. Dad and Mom were married for 71 years. They, literally, loved each other to death. We watched how Dad cared for Mom, during the years they were together, but it was most significant how Dad showed his love for Mom during their last seven years of life together. In those last years before her death, Mom was reduced to silence, but Dad never complained. He would sit beside her for long hours in silence, sometimes muttering a few words and assuming an answer.

In thinking of Dad and Mom's legacy of blessings, I think of Abraham and the words that were said of him in Genesis, "For I have known him, in order that he may command his children and his household after him, that they keep the way of the LORD, to do righteousness and justice, that the LORD may bring to Abraham what He has spoken to him" (Gen. 18:19, NKJV). My siblings and I have never declared Dad and Mom perfect. Like Abraham and Sarah, they had their weaknesses. However, they certainly poured into us blessings that are now flowing out to our children. Even on his deathbed, Dad was still pouring blessings into us.

This book is about sharing the legacy of blessings that God has poured into His children. I am profoundly grateful to write the foreword so I can remind readers that whatever blessings they gather from the book are to be shared. We are all aware that—

> Whatever our hands touch— [knowingly or unknowingly]
> We leave fingerprints!
> On walls, on furniture,
> On doorknobs, dishes, books.
> There's no escape.
> As we touch we leave our identity.
> (Ruth Harms Calkin, *Lord, Could You Hurry a Little?*, p. 79)

May your prayer be:

> *Dear God, wherever I go today, help me leave heart prints!*
> *Heart prints of compassion, love, understanding, and care. Heart prints of kindness, generosity, and genuine concern.*
> *May my heart touch a lonely neighbor, a wayward son or daughter, a neglected student, an anxious mother, someone who has lost a loved one, or perhaps even a friend.*
> *Lord, send us out today to leave heart prints. And if someone should say, "I felt your touch," may that one sense YOUR LOVE touching them through me!*

Let's reach out and make a difference; leave heart prints for Jesus' sake! Leave a positive legacy.

The contents of this book are built from the biblical book of Genesis and are characterized by deep thoughts. They make for healthy meditation. I am convinced that every reader will reap a great harvest of blessings during and after reading.

—Eveythe Cargill, Ph.D., Adjunct Professor,
Calhoun State College, Alabama

Children usually follow the examples of their parents, and that has been profoundly true in my life and in the lives of Carla and Kevin, the two children that God has given to my wife Eveythe and me. My parents owned a home and went the second mile to open it to help others. My wife and I have emulated our parents' example, and we are not surprised that our children are now doing the same. I hope to see our example blossom and replicated in the lives of our grandchildren. Thanks be to God that we are not in a cycle of generational curses but generational blessings.

—Stafford W. Cargill, Ph.D., Associate Professor, Fisk University, Nashville, Tennessee

In celebrating Dr. D. Robert Kennedy in *A Legacy of Blessings*, I join my mother, Dr. Eveythe Cargill, who wrote the foreword, in affirming the legacy of faith that she received from her parents. My parents shared that legacy with my brother and me. My husband and I are now sharing that same legacy with our children—a legacy of faith. This faith has been shared through four generations of my family, which is the greatest gift my husband and I could pass on to our children.

—Dr. Carla Sandy, MD, FACOG, Chief of Gynecology, DC, and Suburban MD, Mid-Atlantic Permanente Medical Group

When I think of *A Legacy of Blessings*, as it has impacted my family, I reflect on the manifested kindness coming through from my grandparents and parents, which has been shared with my sister, Dr. Carla Cargill Sandy, and me and which my wife and I are now making certain to implant in our children. Yes, I have seen those who my mother and father served now returning the kindness during my mother's time of recovery from brain surgery. Truly, as we read in *A Legacy of Blessings*, "kindness begets kindness."

—Kevin Cargill, MBA, CPA, CFO, Adventist Health Care, White Oak Medical Center, Silver Spring, Maryland

The Genesis of Blessings

In the beginning God created the heavens and the earth. (Gen. 1:1, NKJV)

> "Before original sin there was original blessing" (Mark Batterson, Double Blessing, p. 2). That means that, although sin came in, God put in place a plan to continue His blessing. And we need to be thankful for that plan.

1.
The Genesis of Blessings

The story of Genesis has always been an interesting one for me. I read it often, for it helps me to contemplate the mystery of earth's origin and the manifold blessings that God has offered for human happiness. In its introduction, I take note of the fact that God gave us light and life, the sun, moon and stars, and evenings and mornings so we can sleep and wake up to work. He also made the atmosphere with fresh air to breathe. Besides these, God created the sky where birds and airplanes fly. He made numerous species of animals, plants, grains, and multiple sources of food. He made the waters of the seas, rivers, ponds, and aquafers. Above all, God made humanity in His image. He declared all that He had made "good" and "very good." Then God rested from all His work by creating the Sabbath for human delight. In the brief introduction of the Creation story in Genesis 1:1–2:3, we see that God "blessed" the earth three times. First, He blessed the animals (Gen. 1:22), then He blessed humanity (Gen. 1:28), and then He blessed the Sabbath (Gen. 2:3). These are just some of the foundational blessings that God lavished on the earth at the origin of the Creation. After the Fall, multiple curses were pronounced on the planet and on humanity. As one author has put it, in the story of Adam and Eve, "blessing gives way to cursing, as God pronounces the punishments that will blight the lives of Adam and Eve and their descendants" (Gen. 3:16–19). The curses upon humanity brought "hardship for both man and woman" (T. Desmond Alexander, "Blessing and Cursing," available at https://www.ligonier.org/learn/articles/blessing-and-cursing). Thus, man's sin affected the entire creation.

As is the trajectory in all of Scripture, the story told in the Genesis account is an admixture of blessings and curses. However, in Genesis, there is also the record of the exceptional plan that God put in place to restore the blessings on the earth and to all humanity (see Gen. 3:15; 12:1–3).

> *We need to speak more of the copious blessings with which God has favored us.*

In this collection of reflections from "The Pastor's Heart," my op-eds from the *Local Talk* newspaper in New Jersey, I focus on the blessings because too often as human beings we place all our focus on the curses on nature and thus lose sight of the multitudinous blessings that God has bestowed on us. Yes, we need to speak more of the copious blessings with which God has favored us. Looking at my life, I testify that God has poured blessing after blessing on me. As such, I like to offer praise just as the Apostle Paul did in a moment of his reflection when he said:

> Praise be to the God and Father of our Lord Jesus Christ, who has blessed us in the heavenly realms with every spiritual blessing in Christ. For he chose us in him before the creation of the world to be holy and blameless in his sight. In love he predestined us for adoption to sonship through Jesus Christ, in accordance with his pleasure and will—to the praise of his glorious grace, which he has freely given us in the One he loves. (Eph. 1:3–6, NIV)

Anyone who will spend time reading this book should be aware that Genesis is only a starting point for the subject because from Genesis to the last book of the Bible the message is the same: God is profoundly generous with His blessings. In the face of human rebellion, God still finds a way to bestow His blessings. The original blessings are available to all people of the earth even today.

No effort has been made in these reflections to engage in a technical study of Genesis as if one were seeking to write a scholarly document. The primary intent is simply to draw attention to the generosity of God. While humanity continually finds ways to bring on curses, God always finds ways to turn the curses into blessings. As such, we need to appreciate the love by which God shares His blessings with us. Each blessing reminds us of the value that God has put upon us. When God blesses us, we are profoundly blessed, and then He calls on us to become conduits of blessings to others. This is what is meant when we read, "And the LORD had blessed Abraham in all things" (Gen. 24:1, NKJV). But remember that this blessing was preceded by the promise, "All the families of the earth will be blessed through you" (Gen. 12:3, MSG; see also Gen. 22:18; 28:14).

Yes, the reflections in this compilation are just a few of the blessings available to us. Anyone faithful to God has the assurance of such blessings. To all who are willing to be trustworthy, God stands by His word, "I will ... open the windows of heaven for you and pour down for you a blessing until there is no more need [or room to receive]" (Mal. 3:10, ESV).

Take a Moment

Write down any blessing that the above reading has brought to your mind today and for which you would wish to thank the Lord.

_____
_____
_____
_____
_____
_____

Further, write down a special blessing that you would wish to ask the Lord to give you.

_____
_____
_____
_____
_____
_____

Then, write down how and with whom you would wish to share your blessing.

_____
_____
_____
_____
_____
_____

The Legacy of Blessings

So God created man in His own image; in the image of God He created him; male and female He created them. Then God blessed them, and God said to them, "Be fruitful and multiply; fill the earth and subdue it; have dominion over the fish of the sea, over the birds of the air, and over every living thing that moves on the earth." (Gen. 1:27, 28, NKJV)

> Even though God intends His blessings for us all, He cannot give us blessings if we are not ready to receive them and pass them along to others. By sharing with others, we increase our blessings.

2.

The Legacy of Blessings

Even though I might have known it, I kept asking what the word "blessed" means. I have been asking this because, these days, I hear the word tossed about quite tritely. Yes, people say, "God bless you," without giving the expression much thought. They use it as a good luck charm. They say it as a way for people to avoid losing their breath when they sneeze. If the latter is your idea of blessing, then please note that your view is different from the Genesis idea. As I read in the Genesis account, the word "blessing" (*barak*) is rather distinctive. Inserted in His creation plan, God offered His initial blessings on the earth and on humanity to set the basis of all blessings:

> So God created man in His own image; in the image of God He created him; male and female He created them. Then God blessed them, and God said to them, "Be fruitful and multiply; fill the earth and subdue it; have dominion over the fish of the sea, over the birds of the air, and over every living thing that moves on the earth" (Gen. 1:27, 28, NKJV).

The blessings were not just like saying, "I wish you good luck." They had to do with the bestowing, on the earth and all humanity, of God's "favor," "honor," "kindness," "goodness," "justice," and "wisdom." Otherwise stated, God placed in the creation plan His presence, peace, power, provisions, protection, preservation, providence, purpose, and promises. Such blessings are visible and invisible, material and spiritual, emotional and social. A verse and chorus of a song I sing says:

> All things bright and beautiful, all creatures great and small.
> All things wise and wonderful, the Lord God made them all....
> He gave us eyes to see them, and lips that we might tell,
> How great is God Almighty, who has made all things well.
> (Cecil F. Alexander, "All Things Bright and Beautiful")

The point is that, while commentators, at times, have struggled to define the blessings, they seem to agree that, in each blessing, God placed His goodness so that the earth and humanity are not under an eternal state of chaos. As we continue reading the Genesis blessings, we note that, at the beginning, three blessings were offered: (1) the gift of fruitfulness, (2) the gift of procreation, and (3) the gift of stewarding the earth. The three gifts are noted as the root of all other blessings. From the root, the tree of blessings grows and spreads its branches to produce blessings everywhere. Here is what I draw from the root of the first blessings:

1. God is in the business of blessing—He is the giver of all blessings.
2. Blessing is God's default setting—He is waiting to bless.
3. There is no limit to the blessings that God has for humanity.
4. Before original sin there were original blessings.
5. God's blessing is not just the opening act in Genesis, it is also God's providential action in the history of the world.
6. The first blessings of God set the tone for all His blessings.
7. God has covenanted to bless all humanity, and He is faithful to what He has promised.
8. God wants us to find delight—to be blessed—with every blessing.
9. The access to the blessings is based on obedience to the divine command.
10. God's blessings are increased by a life of faith and not fear.
11. God's blessings are multidimensional—you get them in varied forms.
12. God's blessings are uniquely fitted to each person's capacity.
13. It is not easy to quantify or qualify the blessings of God.
14. God's blessings are made operational in us and through us.
15. God's blessings come to us because of what Christ has done.
16. Those who are blessed need to value each blessing.
17. Those most blessed are those who keep close to God.
18. The blessings of God are intended to bring wholeness to us.
19. God's blessings are to be held with an open hand; they are ours to hold, not to hoard.
20. By sharing the blessings of God with others, we increase our blessings.
21. Only with the blessings of God can the world move forward.
22. Those who are blessed of God must be open to God so that God can pour more blessings upon them.
23. The ultimate blessing of life is God.

24. God is doing all that He can do to bless us—even when we mess up, God does all that He can do to turn our missteps into blessings.

> *Before original sin there were original blessings.*

In reading through Genesis, one will find that the book has 48 of the occurrences of the word "blessed" out of the 305 total times the word occurs in the Bible (using the KJV). And, though the blessings have been counteracted by curses, God has found ways to continue the blessings. This is why we find, in the closing book of the Bible, that all the blessings will be restored without interruption. As John declared, "There shall be no more curse" (Rev. 22:3, KJV).

Take a Moment

Write down any blessing that the above reading has brought to your mind today and for which you would wish to thank the Lord.

_____
_____
_____
_____
_____
_____

Further, write down a special blessing that you would wish to ask the Lord to give you.

_____
_____
_____
_____
_____
_____

Then, write down how and with whom you would wish to share your blessing.

_____
_____
_____
_____
_____
_____

The Blessings of Marriage

Therefore a man shall leave his father and mother and be joined to his wife, and they shall become one flesh. (Gen. 2:24, NKJV)

> "Marriage is a blessing; it guards the purity and happiness of the race, it provides for man's social needs, it elevates the physical, the intellectual, and the moral nature." (Ellen G. White, *The Adventist Home*, p. 26)

3.

The Blessings of Marriage

Marriage is one of the first great blessings that God gave to humanity. It is the cradle through which humanity is able to enjoy the cycles of life's greatest blessings. The Scriptures state that God celebrated the first marriage. He declared, "Therefore a man shall leave his father and mother and be joined to his wife, and they shall become one flesh" (Gen. 2:24, NKJV). The writer of Hebrews says, "Marriage is honorable among all, and the bed undefiled; but fornicators and adulterers God will judge" (Heb. 13:4, NKJV). In effect, marriage is part of the order of creation. It is holy. It is good. It is favored by God; it leads to some of life's greatest joys. As we have been told, "When the divine principles are recognized and obeyed in this relation, marriage is a blessing; it guards the purity and happiness of the race, it provides for man's social needs, it elevates the physical, the intellectual, and the moral nature" (Ellen G. White, *The Adventist Home*, p. 25).

Please do not ask those who have gone through some of the most miserable marriages or other forms of broken family relationships to speak of their blessings, for it is the devil's plan to make of a curse anything that God wishes to bless. As my friend Dr. Robert O. A. Samms states in his book, *Paradigms of Marriage*, a marriage can lead to the *pit* or to *paradise*. The *pit*, as it is understood, is hell, the place for the curses, while *paradise* is heaven, the place of blessings. A blessed marriage is the quintessential metaphor of heaven while we are on earth.

To inherit the blessings of marriage we need to focus on what God built into the order of creation. Here are the blessings of marriage that I note:

The oneness. The unitive force is with one man and one woman. "The two shall be one flesh" (Matt. 19:5, NASB). "They are no more two, but one flesh" (Matt. 19:6, ASV). "What God hath joined together, let not man put asunder" (Mark 10:9, ASV). The oneness begins at the initial stage of the marriage but gets closer as couples grow together. Any changing of the creation order creates a challenge for the couple. Anyone who tries to make marriage into a threesome enters into brokenness. The only valid threesome is when the first or third person is God.

The companionship. Oneness does not mean that in the intimacy of a relationship that an individual will lose their individuality. It means that individuals will live interdependently. Here, more than in any other context, we can sing the words of John Fawcett's hymn, "We share our mutual woes, our mutual burdens bear, and often for each other flows the sympathizing tear" (John Fawcett, "Blest Be the Tie That Binds").

The life of holiness. Understand that marriage offers us the opportunity to live in a holy—consecrated—sacred space. God is in the center to make of the relationship a temple. The closer a couple is with God the closer they grow together in holiness.

The Covenantal life. Marriage calls us to a covenant life. That is a life in which two parties vow and pledge to dedicate their lives to be one with the other. A marriage covenant is an agreement between two parties, each seeking the other's interests. So, a husband will look after the interests of his wife; parents will look after the interests of their children; and a believer in Christ will look after the interests of the others in the community of believers of which he or she is a part.

The delightfulness. It is said that the single most robust fact about marriage across many surveys is that married people are happier than anyone else. It is not just a discovery of science. It was the divine intent from the creation. "The LORD God said, 'It is not good for the man to be alone. I will make a helper suitable for him' " (Gen. 2:18, NIV).

> *It is said that the single most robust fact about marriage across many surveys is that married people are happier than anyone else.*

The mutual respect. Here is the context in which neither party is seeking to dominate the other. Both parties in the covenant fully appreciate the mutuality of the relationship. They are different beings, but they give up all self-interest and together become one in mind and spirit. The statement, "Wives, be subject to your husbands, as is fitting in the Lord" (Col. 3:18, NASB), is balanced by the statement, "Husbands, love your wives, as Christ loved the church" (Eph. 5:25).

The sharing of love. Marriage offers the most effective context to understand all the dimensions of love—friendship love (*philos*), erotic love (*eros*), sacrificial love (*agap*), and parental or nurturing love (*st rge*). We were not born loving; we learn to love, and marriage is intended to be the most intimate environment in which love can be tested and can grow.

The challenging of self-centeredness. If you are a self-centered person, you will undoubtedly have a miserable marriage. This is why divorce, infidelity, and sexual relations outside of marriage have traditionally been frowned upon as abrogating the sacredness of marriage. This is why after its comment on the "honorableness" of marriage, Hebrews tells us that "whoremongers and adulterers God will judge" (Heb. 13:4, KJV).

The rearing of a family. Marriage creates the ideal context in which to raise a healthy family. The brokenness that our children are experiencing today was never intended by God. When two people work together as a team to rear a child, the child experiences more balanced relationships.

Support. Marriage is the place where human beings find the best support. It is the context in which one can be most vulnerable with their love, burdens, pleasures, and the sharing of secrets.

Self-enrichment. Marriage is the context for knowing who you are. You learn by sharing with your alter ego, a person who is your secondary or alternative personality, your intimate and trusted friend. Such a person can challenge you, "criticize" you, and help you know who you are and how you can better yourself.

Safe sex. Talk about a context for safe sex: it is in marriage. You hold the union as a sacred space where you can walk around naked without feeling that you are going to be raped or abused. In every way, here is where you can show that, despite your bulge, you are appreciated.

Spiritual stimulation. It is said that marriage is the relationship that best mirrors the spirituality of the divine. In marriage, the dual characteristics of God—His masculine and feminine aspects—are harmonized as one. Marriage seeks to open up our better understanding of life by turning us to God.

The building of trust. We learn to trust by exploring our most intimate relationships. When a woman says, "I do not trust men," or men say, "I don't trust women," it is mostly because they have not had the opportunity to build trust in their most significant relationship. Psychologist Lori Gordon describes conjugal love as enabling you "to feel that you can trust another person with your whole being, your laughter, your tears, your rage, your joy . . . . Its essence lies in total certainty that your partner is emotionally fully there with you and for you—open to you in body, heart, and mind—and knowing that you can offer the same to your partner. It's the ability to lower your defenses and share yourself fully with another human being, knowing that you are accepted and loved for what you are, and knowing that you don't have to pretend."

Giving and receiving. It is said, "It is more blessed to give than to receive" (Acts 20:35, NKJV). God has created marriage as the context for both giving and receiving. If one partner is always giving and never receiving, that partner will never have enough to give. In effect, marriage is a two-way relationship in which we learn to give and receive.

Communication. Effective relationships are built on communication. You share a language that is the instrument for building the relationship. Words matter. Sweet words strengthen the bones. Sour words hurt. God intended that we base our words to affirm each other.

Enhanced health. Ask doctors and other scientists, their research has demonstrated that married people tend to live longer than single people. I was reading one article that says, "A major survey of 127,545 American adults found that married men are healthier than men who were never married or whose marriages ended in divorce or widowhood. Men who have marital partners also live longer than men without spouses; men who marry after age 25 get more protection than those who tie the knot at a younger age. The longer a man stays married, the greater his survival advantage over his unmarried peers. But is marriage itself responsible for better health and a longer life?" ("Marriage and Men's Health," first published July 2010, updated June 5, 2019, available at https://www.health.

harvard.edu/mens-health/marriage-and-mens-health). Do I need to find the research on women as well? Indeed not, but imagine that the studies reveal the same. It would be nice to be in a perfect world where all married couples are healthier, but the challenges that are faced are so profound that many marriages make people sicker.

Budgeting. At an average marriage offers the best context to manage a budget. One person might be a better money manager than the other and thus they can share their strengths. Solomon says, "Two are better than one, because they have a good reward for their labor. For if they fall, one will lift up his companion. But woe to him who is alone when he falls, for he has no one to help him up" (Eccles. 4:9, 10, NKJV).

Glorifying God. Our marriages are intended to bring glory to God. That means any marriage that stands under the sovereignty of God, reflecting the divine character of love, holiness, purity, grace, justice, and all that is of God, glorifies God. If a person chooses to get married, such a person must decide on whether the purpose of marriage is to bring glory to self or to God. Only in this way can the marriage be a channel of blessings to the couple and to the generations that come from the marriage.

In anticipation of the heavenly life. Yes, marriage is not intended to keep our minds in this world but to be a symbol of our heavenly life. A blessed marriage is a symbol of the church on earth and the church in heaven (Eph. 5:22–32). I am not sure how to explain the concept that, in heaven, we shall live like angels, but I am looking forward to meeting with and being with my wife at the great Messianic banqueting table (Matt. 22:30; Rev. 19:9).

Take a Moment

Write down any blessing that the above reading has brought to your mind today and for which you would wish to thank the Lord.

_____
_____
_____
_____
_____
_____

Further, write down a special blessing that you would wish to ask the Lord to give you.

_____
_____
_____
_____
_____
_____

Then, write down how and with whom you would wish to share your blessing.

_____
_____
_____
_____
_____
_____

The Blessings of Children

God blessed them and said to them, "Be fruitful and increase in number; fill the earth and subdue it. Rule over the fish in the sea and the birds in the sky and over every living creature that moves on the ground." (Gen. 1:28, NIV)

> "Children derive life and being from their parents, and yet it is through the creative power of God that your children have life, for God is the Life-giver. Let it be remembered that children are not to be treated as though they were our own personal property. Children are the heritage of the Lord, and the plan of redemption includes their salvation as well as ours. They have been entrusted to parents in order that they might be brought up in the nurture and admonition of the Lord, that they might be qualified to do their work in time and eternity." (Ellen G. White, *Adventist Home*, p. 280)

4.

The Blessings of Children

One evening I was watching the news on CNN, and, at the moment of exchange between Anderson Cooper and Chris Cuomo, Cooper showed a picture of his newborn baby. Cuomo gave Cooper an exceptional compliment and then said something to the effect, "Cooper, watch and see, how your life is going to change. A child or children will do that to you." On noticing the pleasure on Cooper's face, I reflexively asked: "Cooper, who is the mother?" I knew he could not hear me, and I was glad because I knew of his lifestyle choice. I then scolded myself for reacting as I did. After my initial reaction, I acknowledged that the child was a precious baby. And I agreed that the child will undoubtedly make Cooper into a different person, as Cuomo said, for I know from experience that children will do that to you.

I have heard quite a few parents complaining about how burdened they feel under Covid-19 because their children have had to stay at home. When they have to supervise their children's schoolwork on Zoom or other platforms and organize the multiple activities in which their children engage to pass their time at home, it is stressful. Many parents are complaining that the pressures are truly getting to them. There is also the report that the stresses are causing some parents to abuse their children. Some social workers have reported that child abuse is up. It seems that more attention is being paid to the situations of children today. In our contemporary society, the attitude about children is not as it should be. In some societies of the past, children were valued. Thus, for example, the Psalmist calls them the "heritage of the LORD" (Ps. 127:3, KJV). But as people turned away from God, their attitude about children changed and children were valued more for their economic benefit than for the multiple blessings that they bring to a family and the world. As Jesus came along, He sought to affirm the original high regard for children. He made it clear that, if anyone should cause a child to stumble, it would be better for a millstone to be put upon his neck and he be cast into the bottom of the ocean (see Matt. 18:6; Luke 17:1, 2).

For some parents today, children are counted as a bother because they get in the way of career and professional attainments. Pursuit of a career is one of the biggest reasons that so many children are aborted. And many that are brought to full term are neglected, abused, and abandoned. Many are caught in the crossfires of divorce, even being left to provide emotional support for their divorced parents. One has to wonder how many of us really see children as a blessing.

Despite the grim picture we see painted, it is notable that there are many parents who see children as blessings. Thus, after listening to that interchange between Anderson Cooper and Chris Cuomo on the night I referenced above, I kept on thinking about the subject, and, in a few days, I heard Andrew Cuomo, the Governor of New York, boasting about his daughters. I hastened home to talk with my wife about the blessings upon our children. Then I began to list blessings that we have had with our children, and I came up with the following thirty blessings:

1. Our children have given us joy, pleasure, and enjoyment in our souls.
2. They have brought wonder to our hearts; they make us wonder concerning the miracle of their birth.
3. Their laughter is like sweet music to our ears.
4. Their play brings stimulation to our lives.
5. Their imagination brings inspiration to our minds.
6. Their hugs have made us think we are profoundly special in their world.
7. When they share their stories, they bring us delight.
8. Receiving their appreciation for what we did for them thrills our hearts.
9. They are a source of comfort to our lives.
10. They are crowns of rejoicing to our old age.
11. Knowing that they are blood family on whom we can lavish our attention is a wonderful feeling.
12. Seeing their character development brings hope for the future.
13. In them, we know that the future of the family is secure.
14. They bring honor to the family by their positive attitudes.
15. We learn to be right providers of food and shelter to let them know that we care.
16. They prompt us to be protective as we make sure they are safe and healthy.
17. They cause us to know the power of example.

18. They teach us how to be creative.
19. They teach us new skills: We gain areas of expertise that we never had before, such as fixing their bike chain when it falls off or learning something about social media to keep them safe.

> *Their hugs have made us think we are profoundly special in their world.*

20. They teach us patience. As someone has said, children "subdue the traits of our character."
21. They teach us to be persistent.
22. We learn perseverance in challenging situations. When our children get sick, we persevere until we see them getting better.
23. They help us build an unrelenting prayer life.
24. We develop empathy (EQ).
25. Through them, we see potential and possibility in everyone.
26. We build trust in them and learn to trust others.
27. By their successes and failures, we learn humility.
28. We learn to build connections for them and give support to others.
29. They teach us how to deal with our anxieties and our fears; even if it is to play brave, we often act with courage to protect them.
30. We share with them our faith and see them passing it on to the next generation.

It is a tragedy that not all children bring such blessings. Yet, from the beginning of time, God intended that children bring blessings. For this reason, He gave the command with the utmost encouragement, "Be fruitful and increase in number; fill the earth and subdue it" (Gen. 1:28, NIV). One has to be impressed concerning the blessings children bring when one reads the book of Genesis and the other parts of the Bible. One cannot miss how distressed many women felt when they could not have children and how they considered it God's favor when children came. (Compare the stories of Sarah, in Genesis 17; of Rachel, in Genesis 30; and of Hannah, in 1 Samuel 1.) The Bible also tells of the judgment that God will bring against any person or society that does not take care of their children (Matt. 18:6; Mark 9:42; Luke 17:17). The Bible also bemoans the father or mother who does not give special attention to their children (1 Tim. 5:8; Isa. 49:15), and it takes note of how God offers special attention to the fatherless (Deut. 10:18; James 2:15–17).

Yes, God has given us multiple blessings through our children, and He has given us numerous privileges so we can pass on our blessings. In this way, our children will be able to live out their blessings instead of living under curses. As the Psalmist says, "Behold, children are a heritage from the LORD, the fruit of the womb is a reward. Like arrows in the hand of a warrior, so are the children of one's youth. Happy is the man who has his quiver full of them; They shall not be ashamed, but shall speak with their enemies in the gate" (Ps. 127:3–5, NKJV).

It is a tragedy that we so often turn the blessings of our children into curses. So, let us pray that God will help us to be wise enough to turn our attention to the preserving of these blessings. A thought I often quote from the great reformer John Calvin is: "All the blessings we enjoy are Divine deposits, committed to our trust on this condition, that they should be dispensed for the benefit of our neighbors."

Take a Moment

Write down any blessing that the above reading has brought to your mind today and for which you would wish to thank the Lord.

_____
_____
_____
_____
_____
_____

Further, write down a special blessing that you would wish to ask the Lord to give you.

_____
_____
_____
_____
_____
_____

Then, write down how and with whom you would wish to share your blessing.

_____
_____
_____
_____
_____
_____

The Blessings of Family

Then God blessed them, and God said to them, "Be fruitful and multiply; fill the earth and subdue it; have dominion over the fish of the sea, over the birds of the air, and over every living thing that moves on the earth." (Gen. 1:28, NKJV)

> "The family tie is the closest, the most tender and sacred, of any on earth. It was designed to be a blessing to mankind. And it is a blessing wherever the marriage covenant is entered into intelligently, in the fear of God, and with due consideration for its responsibilities." (Ellen G. White, *Adventist Home*, p. 18)

5.

The Blessings of Family

At a time the world is involved in social distancing and staying-at-home measures, a number of people are saying that they are finding it difficult to establish new love relationships or to keep family together. Many who are looking for love have no family. As we have heard, "The family tie is the closest, the most tender and sacred, of any on earth. It was designed to be a blessing to mankind. And it is a blessing wherever the marriage covenant is entered into intelligently, in the fear of God, and with due consideration for its responsibilities" (Ellen G. White, *The Ministry of Healing*, pp. 356, 357).

While shopping at the start of the Coronavirus pandemic, although I knew there was a state order in force, I could not help but noticing how many people around me were wearing masks. I myself was wearing two masks, the second added by my wife who felt that she needed to make me extra secure. A few people, I noticed, were not wearing any mask, but about 99% of the shoppers and clerks were wearing them. While standing in the checkout line, my mind began to wonder, and my boyish self told me to ask an older woman, who was standing closest to me, what might she have done if she were looking for a special (boy)friend at this time. I did not dare ask, however, because, on second thought, I felt she would think me impolite. Yet, the question, I think, is pertinent since it has been established that, when people are under stress, it often affects their capacity for finding friends or building family.

An article in *Psychology Today* entitled, "How Stress Can Bury Love," states that, because of COVID 19, people's senses—touch, smell, taste, sight, hearing, and intuition, by which they experience the world and those around them, are compromised. That is, when the senses are undermined, so is the ability to connect intimately. The writer asks us to imagine ourselves being so exhausted and pressured that we have no energy to respond to our partner's needs, let alone take in what such a partner may offer. Because we may be burnt out, our partner will face a different kind of burnout, namely, he or she may be trying to awaken us from our internalized focus. As psychologist Randi Gunther has stated, "Intimate partners become discouraged when their lovers suffer prolonged stress, and they stop trying to get the relationship back on track if their frustrations grow too painful to endure" (Randi Gunther, Ph.D., "How Stress Can Bury Love – The Way Back," available at https://www.psychologytoday.com/us/blog/rediscovering-love/201411/how-stress-can-bury-love-the-way-back). They may go through emotions of uncertainty, confusion, anger, and distress as they try to deal with their frustrations until they still come to the realization that nothing they do can bring the kind of resolution that they might wish.

Yes, we are being told that, in our time of dealing with COVID 19 and social distancing, that—

1   Tensions between spouses are at an all-time high. One comment I have read states: "Just what we need: A new source of family division as we clash over how to properly respond to a killer pandemic when millions of American families are shut in for maybe months and already getting on each other's nerves" (Maria Puente, "Family feud: Clashing over coronavirus is the new source of household tension, fighting," *USA Today*, April 9, 2020).
2. Separation and divorce are on the rise. One newspaper headline declares: "China's divorce rates rise as couples emerge from coronavirus quarantine" (Sheridan Prasso, "China's Divorce Spike Is a Warning to Rest of Locked-Down World," March 31, 2020, available at https://www.bloomberg.com/news/articles/2020-03-31/divorces-spike-in-china-after-coronavirus-quarantines). The conclusion is: "Although China publishes nationwide statistics on divorce only annually, media reports from various cities show uncoupling surged in March as husbands and wives began emerging from weeks of government-mandated lockdowns intended to stop the spread of the novel coronavirus. Incidents of domestic violence also multiplied. The trend may be an ominous warning for couples in the U.S. and elsewhere who are in the early stages of isolating at home: If absence makes the heart grow fonder, the opposite might be true of too much time spent together in close quarters."
3. More children are being abused than usual. One news network frames it, "Children may be at an increased risk for abuse and neglect in quarantine" (Abby Cruz and Elizabeth Thomas,

"Children may be at an increased risk for abuse and neglect in quarantine: Experts," available at https://abcnews.go.com/Health/children-increased-risk-abuse-neglect-quarantine-experts/story?id=70041839).
4. Families and friends are stressed because they cannot visit their loved ones, even while some have been in hospitals facing death. They cannot be there to hold their hands. Families and friends cannot celebrate birthdays in their usual ways.
5. Spiritual life is easily challenged, even as many families face sickness and death. Many who experience grief, shock, anxiety, fear, sadness, powerlessness, anger, and helplessness wonder where God is. Such feelings and many others are normal to all humanity. But when families confront negative situations, while they declare their faith in God, their faith can be severely tested. In the midst of the test, a mother or father might ask, "Where is God when my child is dying?" Or "What is God doing as a member of the family faces an unexpected diagnosis?" The family might have prayed and waited for God for a long time, but, when expected miracles do not happen, the questions begin to flow. Yet, after the questions, some families do settle that, for whatever time they are able to spend with loved ones, it was God who brought such wonderful blessings into the family.

Reflecting on the conditions my own family has faced, I have put together a list of blessings, which I often share as I speak to families in distress. Here they are:

1. It is said that love of family is life's greatest blessing, for the love that is shared is a special kind of love. It includes the love (*störge*) between parent and child, the love (*philos*) between siblings, the love (*eros*) between spouses, and the love (*agape*) between the family and God. When the love of God is shared in the family, it binds everyone together.
2. A second great blessing of family is that of being able to laugh together and cry together amid pain. In joy or in sorrow, a family is there for each other.
3. The family provides a circle that influences the development of one's faith.
4. It also provides a circle in which one can be most vulnerable with one's burdens of life.

> *A second great blessing of family is that of being able to laugh together and cry together amid pain.*

5. It is also that circle that comes to your rescue when others might be socially distanced from you.
6. It is the circle in which individualism is downplayed and community building is emphasized.
7. The family is the one circle in which we are primarily nurtured.
8. It is the circle in which we can be best challenged to be most accountable.
9. It is the circle that allows us the best environment for safety and protection.
10. It is the circle that best affirms and encourages or cheers us along life's path.
11. It is the circle that best offers the hugs and cuddling that are needed for our survival.
12. The family is the natural circle that is created to be our nurturing center.
13. It is the circle in which everyone knows our name.
14. It is the circle in which we can be best prepared for life.
15. It is the circle in which we learn the responsibility of contributing to each other's emotional and spiritual well-being.
16. It is the circle in which we learn what are often the most useful values of our lives.
17. It is the circle in which those who are aging are best protected.
18. It is the circle for preserving the future of civilization.

It is so very sad that so many families do not have a tight circle, for blessings are best passed within that circle. If you do not have a family, it is good to begin to build one by taking time to love those about you. They may not be your birth family, but they will be part of the most intimate circle on which you can depend.

Now, if you are asking or looking for practical ways in which to build and share your love with your family during the present time of Covid-19, let me offer the following list of 20 suggestions for you to consider—

1. Put aside any pride and selfishness in your heart because they will kill your love.
2. Seek to build up trust with those about you. Trust builds love.

3. Be compassionate. Find ways of doing thoughtful things.
4. Be kind, and speak kindly. Shop for someone who might need your help and leave the order on their steps to let them pick it up.
5. Be respectful. Respect engenders respect.
6. Be patient if tempers flare about you.
7. Do not take yourself too seriously. I have told many individuals that, if you are too serious about life, life will take you dead serious.
8. Avoid criticism and attack language—putting others down destroys love.
9. Send someone a card with a comforting message.
10. Phone, Facetime, or Zoom your loved ones, even your distant friends. A voice is sometimes better than a text.

> *If you are too serious about life, life will take you dead serious.*

11. Share a movie together, and even recommend one to your friends.
12. Send a text message or a WhatsApp message to those with whom you can be connected. You may even send something cheerful to those who are very near to you. Yet, do not overwhelm them with text or WhatsApp messages. Do not forward fake stories.
13. Pray and worship together. When you go to God together, you will become closer together.
14. Call and pray with a friend, or read a passage of Scripture or an inspirational thought together. People who live by themselves especially appreciate such calls.
15. Share fresh protective masks with others if you know where to purchase them or how to make them. Find out how you can help.
16. Play games with another person and build a relationship.
17. Go out to safe spaces and walk in the sun together. Practice safe distancing.
18. Learn the power of forgiveness. We all make mistakes, but, when we forgive, we build love.
19. Ask the Lord to help you use your creativity to do loving things.
20. Loving is doing something good for others.

The Apostle John writes, "Dear friends, let us love one another, for love comes from God. Everyone who loves has been born of God and knows God. Whoever does not love does not know God, because God is love. This is how God showed his love among us: He sent his one and only Son into the world that we might live through him" (1 John 4:7–9, NIV). The Danish philosopher Soren Kierkegaard wrote: "Worldly wisdom thinks that love is a relationship between man and woman. Christianity teaches that love is a relationship between man-God-woman, that is, that God is the middle term."

How do you see it? Does your family relationship put God at the center or is God to the side? At the beginning of time, when God established the family, God visited the family in the garden in the cool of the day, and this is what God intends even to the end. God wants to be at the center of your family.

Take a Moment

Write down any blessing that the above reading has brought to your mind today and for which you would wish to thank the Lord.

_____
_____
_____
_____
_____
_____

Further, write down a special blessing that you would wish to ask the Lord to give you.

_____
_____
_____
_____
_____
_____

Then, write down how and with whom you would wish to share your blessing.

_____
_____
_____
_____
_____
_____

The Blessings of Sabbath Rest

Thus the heavens and the earth, and all the host of them, were finished. And on the seventh day God ended His work which He had done, and He rested on the seventh day from all His work which He had done. Then God blessed the seventh day and sanctified it, because in it He rested from all His work which God had created and made. (Gen. 2:1–3, NKJV)

> God constantly offers us His blessings, but we can be so blind and deaf that we do not welcome them. Sabbath blessings are among the greatest blessings. The Sabbath should be celebrated and not rejected.

6.

The Blessings of Sabbath Rest

Can you believe that, before human beings ever worked a single day, God gave them a day of rest? (See Gen. 1:26; 2:1–3; Mark 2:27, 28.) Before scientists came along to make the most profound discoveries concerning rest, God had settled it that human beings are ever in need of physical, mental, emotional, and spiritual rest. God knew that, in order for us to gain or renew our strength, deepen our meditation, increase our productivity, nurture our inspiration, enjoy happiness, find healing, and share the finest blessings of life, we needed rest. I do not mean only the rest of sleep or of a holiday, but Sabbath rest—the rest by which we take a break from work to pursue the things that lead to our soul's development. When human beings fail to listen to the divine prescriptions for such rest, their lives are thrown out of balance.

This is why, after giving human beings, in the garden of Eden, the first great blessing of **marriage and the family** (Gen. 1:26–28; see also 2:18–25), God gave humanity the second great blessing of *Sabbath rest*. In Genesis 2, we find the story: "Thus the heavens and the earth were completed in all their vast array. By the seventh day God had finished the work he had been doing; so on the seventh day he rested from all his work." Then "God blessed the seventh day and made it holy, because on it he rested from all the work of creating that he had done" (Gen. 2:1–3, NIV).

What a gift is the blessing of Sabbath rest! At the end of the creation week, God stopped working and He rested. This action stands in dramatic contrast to what is reported of the pagan gods who never rested. In the pagan stories, the gods work and work until they burn out, self-destruct, and become an artifact of history. However, in the biblical story, God rested and blessed the Sabbath, making it a day of holy pleasure for all humanity. That He created the Sabbath before the existence of sin tells us that Sabbath should not be a burden. It was not to be seen in connection with whether we have worked and gotten tired because of any sinful condition. Although the Sabbath is to be a boundary for

> *That He created the Sabbath before the existence of sin tells us that Sabbath should not be a burden.*

our work schedule (see Exod. 20:8–11), the Sabbath has a greater purpose than our resting from work. The Sabbath is for spiritual relationship building with God, the family, and other human beings. According to the biblical account, God did two great things with the Sabbath that He had not done with the other days of creation.

1. He blessed the Sabbath—that is, He made it a day distinctly favored from every other day.
2. He hallowed, or sanctified, the Sabbath—that is, He set it apart, consecrating it for holy use.

This is why Jesus said, "The Sabbath was made for man, and not man for the Sabbath, Therefore the Son of Man is also Lord of the Sabbath" (Mark 2:27, 28, NKJV).

While human beings have done everything to make the Sabbath like any other day, have sought to secularize the Sabbath and turned it into a work day, and have sought to remove the blessing of the Sabbath, hollowing it out and substituting for it Sunday, the first day of the week, or Friday or other days of the week, the seventh-day Sabbath has remained a perpetual blessing for all the creation. There is no substitute that can effectively replace it. No coffee or energy drink or alcohol or anything else can make up for it. All the substitutes that human beings have tried, have failed because, as the promise says, "What God has blessed no one can curse."

Our point of interest is to ask whether we spurn or value God's blessed day of rest. A survey of the Bible reveals that the Sabbath carries myriad blessings—too many to catalogue. I list the following twenty-five most significant Sabbath blessings for reflection. The Sabbath is—

1. A day of finding holy pleasure in God.
2. A day to rest and admire the creative work of God.
3. A day to fine-tune our minds, to hear God speak more deeply.
4. A day to study the Word of God.
5. A day to set aside for spiritual uplifting and refreshment.
6. A day for the family to meet and share with each other.
7. A day to meet with the community of the faithful.

8. A day for sharing the joy of the Lord.
9. A day of peace when the soul comes to rest from all the temporal burdens of six days in the week.
10. A day of extra-ordinary miracles. Think of the miracles of the manna and the Sabbath miracles of Jesus.
11. A day of delight. Oswald Chambers says that, "The busyness of things [often] obscures our concentration on God."
12. A day of contemplation on the goodness of God.
13. A day of healing heartbreak, injury, and brokenness in relationships.
14. A day of freedom from servitude. Karl Barth said, "A being is free only when it can determine and limit its activity."
15. A day of restoration from a life of sin.
16. A day of deliverance from oppression.
17. A day of grace as freedom from business transaction.
18. A day of faith when all is left in the hands of God.
19. A day of opportunity to bring out the best in our characters.
20. A day to distinguish the holy from the profane and enjoy, as Abraham Joshua Heschel described it, "Holiness in time."
21. A day to experience the intensified manifestation of the presence of God.
22. A day of freedom from economic constraints and a day to return a tithe and offering from the blessings that God has provided.
23. A day of anticipating eternity, which helps us think of eternal Sabbath rest.
24. A day that frees us from the curses of self-centeredness, as Marva Dawn wrote: "Sabbath ceasing [means] to cease . . . from our possessiveness and our enculturation, and, finally, from the humdrum and meaninglessness that result when life is pursued without the Lord at the center of it all" (Marva Dawn, *Keeping the Sabbath Wholly*, 1989, p. 3).
25. A day with a legacy of blessings to share—blessing after blessing, as Matthew Henry wrote: "The streams of religion run deep or shallow, according as the banks of the Sabbath are kept up or neglected."

We make the point that, taken as a whole, the Sabbath brings us the most copious blessings of life. Therefore, we need to appreciate more fully when Sabbath comes each week. We need to be taking time to welcome the Sabbath and pass the blessings that are given by God to those around us.

We need to take time to sing Sabbath songs and read Sabbath Psalms and the rest of Scripture to anticipate our entry into the eternal Sabbath rest. As one hymn writer put it, "When Sabbaths here shall end, and from these courts we move, may we an endless Sabbath spend in heavenly courts above" ("The Sabbath," *Hymns and Tunes*, 1876, no. 90).

Let us strive to enjoy the Edenic Sabbath while anticipating the eternal Sabbath.

Take a Moment

Write down the blessing that the above reading has brought to your mind today and for which you would wish to thank the Lord.

_____
_____
_____
_____
_____
_____

Further, write down a special blessing that you would wish to ask the Lord to give you.

_____
_____
_____
_____
_____
_____

Then, write down how and with whom you would wish to share your blessing.

_____
_____
_____
_____
_____
_____

The Blessings of Work

Then the LORD God took the man and put him in the garden of Eden to tend and keep it. (Gen. 2:15, NKJV)

> It was a fact of great interest when my father, at the age of 95 years of age, was budding and planting fruit trees. One day I asked him why, and he said to me, "If I do not eat from them, somebody else will." I asked no further questions, for I knew what he meant, namely, that the blessings of God are passed on to us to be passed to the third and fourth generations.

7.

The Blessings of Work

A person with whom I shared a copy of my book, *Silence of the Soul*, later texted me to report her appreciation for the gift. She said that she found a blessing in the tragedy of the COVID 19 pandemic because it allowed her to get away from her hectic work schedule and take a little time to read. She noted that the COVID 19 stay-at-home order had allowed her to have "a sabbath rest," and to read the book that had brought her a tremendous blessing.

While I was rejoicing with her, I began to thank God for every blessing that I also had received by working and resting on Sabbath. I haven't had to wait for a pandemic or a time of sickness to rest. Each week I work and look forward to the Sabbath to rest from my toil of the week. Sabbath is no excuse not to work, nor is work an excuse not to keep Sabbath.

After speaking of the blessings of the Sabbath it is good to take note of the blessings of work, for when God created humanity, He gave us work. Or let us say, in the paradisaic life of Eden, work was required.

This is what is stated: "Then the LORD God took the man and put him in the garden of Eden to tend and keep it" (Gen. 2:15, NKJV).

Work was not an afterthought. We are made to work. That is why, from the beginning of time, idleness has been considered a curse. The wise man Solomon has many criticisms about laziness (called in the old KJV "slothfulness"). Read some examples in Proverbs 12:24; 13:4; 15:19; 24:30–34; 21:25). The Apostle Paul calls laziness the devil's workshop (see 2 Thess. 3:11; 1 Tim. 5:13).

God has so made us that we need to work. That is why, during the Covid-19 lockdowns, so many people have been in despair because they cannot get to work. It is unfortunate, I have said, that instead of work being made a blessing it has been turned into a curse.

In the west, we worship work. Many have sought to work twelve hours instead of eight hours per day. Some work for twenty-four hours without rest, until their health and mental wellbeing is destroyed—they are burned out. Some, who do not do all the work themselves, turn those about them into slaves. The point that I am making is that we have not learned to appreciate work. Rather, we worship work instead of worshiping the God who has provided work and given us the strength to work.

As I have had time to reflect during this Covid-19 time, let me state that, while there is a need to get back to work, we must not lose our blessings by being foolish about how we approach work.

Whatever we do for work, we must consider the context of our work. We must ensure that our work allows room for the blessings that God has provided. We need not make our work a drudgery. We need not wait for a sabbatical to appreciate how to balance our work. We need not allow our work to become a curse.

We need to follow the pattern of work that God established when He created the earth. Six days God created, and then, on the seventh day—the sabbath day—God "rested and was refreshed" (Exod. 31:17, KJV). Whatever "refresh" means in the context of the text is not absolutely clear to commentators. They suggest that it must mean that God stood back from His work of creating and "took a breath." He took a moment to admire His work as we need to do so that we can enjoy the blessings of our work. Here are thirty of the greatest blessings I have noted over the years about work.

1. We are Godlike when we work—in creating the earth, God worked (Gen. 1:1ff; John 5:17; 9:4), and we are created to act in a Godlike way as pro-creators (Gen. 2:8–15).
2. God placed us on earth to work, to keep and care for the earth, and to govern its creatures (Gen. 1:26, 28). We are managers of what God has placed on the earth. If we admit the truth, we will have to say that we have turned the blessings of our management into curses.
3. We work to glorify God (1 Tim. 5:8–10). The alternative is that many people use work to glorify themselves, idolizing their work.
4. Work makes us feel good. It gives us a sense of personal satisfaction.
5. Work gives meaning and purpose to our lives. Those who do not work often feel a sense of meaninglessness.
6. Work brings the enjoyment of life and helps us find delight in the Sabbath (Isa. 58:14).
7. Work helps us develop diligence, that is, how to be careful and persistent with our work.

> *Work gives meaning and purpose to our lives.*

8. Work helps us develop discipline, which is the creation of order in our lives.
9. Work helps us develop our character. It impacts the noble qualities that make us who we are. Many people got their name from the work they did. For example, Richard the shoemaker became Richard Shoemaker. John the baker became John Baker.
10. Work helps us provide for our daily necessities. By work, we are able to take care of our families.
11. Work helps us to take advantage of our life's potential. We can admire our work as God did when He worked and called it "good."
12. We work to fill our vocation. It provides us with profit and prosperity (see Prov. 14:4, 23).
13. Work helps us to build memories. Our work experiences influence who we are. We can look back at the product of our work and reflect on what we have done.
14. Work helps us to build good attitudes. This is why we are encouraged to teach children to work.
15. We are to be thankful for the opportunity to work. Some people want to work and cannot find a job. So, when we work, we can be thankful for our work.
16. Work helps us build self-confidence.
17. Work gives us opportunities to render service to others.
18. Work influences how we form our habits.
19. Work helps us to distinguish qualities of excellence.
20. When we work, we build up skills, talents, and gifts.
21. Work helps us strengthen our muscles.
22. Work teaches the value of cooperation or teamwork. Adam and Eve were created to work together. Their work was more effective together than apart. Dr. James Paul Gee emphasizes that whether we are professionals or amateurs, our collective intelligence is better than our individual intelligence. Couples, parents, and children (with chores) do a better job together than alone. (See James Paul Gee, *The Anti-Education Era: Creating Smarter Students Through Digital Learning*, pp. 192, 193)
23. Work helps us build up a sense of responsibility.
24. Work helps us develop physical life. It helps us use our hands, eyes, ears, feet, and other body parts and muscles.

25. Work helps us to build our spiritual wellbeing, which is why the Bible condemns laziness (Prov. 10:4, 5; 12:11, 24; 13:4, etc.).
26. Work brings us inspiration. Inspiration, we know, is fleeting, but it is best sustained when we work. We need to work in an environment where we are inspired rather than in an environment that devalues or depresses us.
27. Work allows us to render service to others (see Eph. 4:28).
28. Through work, we leave artifacts for the next generation.
29. Through work, we transform the world. Proper work makes a positive contribution, while careless work destroys the earth.

In effect, our work only brings blessings when done in God's way. This is why the Scriptures say, "Whatever you do, work at it with all your heart, as working for the Lord, not for human masters, since you know that you will receive an inheritance from the Lord as a reward. It is the Lord Christ you are serving" (Col. 3:23, 24, NIV).

God cares about our work. So, work as if you are working for God. Do not idolize work. Do not overwork. Do not enslave others to do your work. As the Scriptures say, "Six days you shall labor, and do all your work, but the seventh day is a Sabbath to the LORD your God. On it you shall not do any work, you, or your son, or your daughter, your male servant, or your female servant, or your livestock, or the sojourner who is within your gates. For in six days the LORD made heaven and earth, the sea, and all that is in them, and rested on the seventh day. Therefore, the LORD blessed the Sabbath day and made it holy" (Exod. 20: 9–11, ESV).

Also, take time away from work to rest. If ever you are without work, use the time to develop new skills so that you can have flexibility in the way that you work. God never intended that work be a curse. Rather, He intended that it be a blessing, and the blessing comes when we are liberated for rest and relaxation, worship, relationship building, and other facets of life that make for blessings.

There is a powerful story in the book of Luke that tells of an occasion when Jesus visited the home of Mary and Martha. Martha was working as hard as she could to make Jesus feel welcome, while Mary sat at Jesus' feet, taking time to listen to Jesus' teaching. Martha became outraged and went to Jesus to ask Him to send Mary to help her. "And Jesus answered and said to her, 'Martha, Martha, you are worried and troubled about many things. But one thing is needed, and Mary has chosen that good part, which will not be taken away from her' " (Luke 10:41, 42). The lesson for Martha is for all of us as well. While our existence does call us to work, life is more than work. Neale Donald Walsch put it another way in his book, *Conversations with God:* "Your soul cares only about what you are BEING while you are doing whatever you are doing. It is a state of BEINGNESS the soul is after, not a state of doingness."

Take a Moment

Write down the blessing that the above reading has brought to your mind today and for which you would wish to thank the Lord.

_____
_____
_____
_____
_____
_____

Further, write down a special blessing that you would wish to ask the Lord to give you.

_____
_____
_____
_____
_____
_____

Then, write down how and with whom you would wish to share your blessing.

_____
_____
_____
_____
_____
_____

The Blessings of Daily Provisions

God said, "See, I have given you every plant yielding seed that is upon the face of all the earth, and every tree with seed in its fruit; you shall have them for food. And to every beast of the earth, and to every bird of the air, and to everything that creeps on the earth, everything that has the breath of life, I have given every green plant for food." And it was so. (Gen. 1:29, 30, NRSV)

> We are to enjoy the provisions that God has given us. As we use them to bless our lives, we are to share them with others. Robert Morris says, "It is God's will for us to be blessed so we can be a blessing" (*Beyond Blessed*, p. 63).

8.
The Blessings of Daily Provisions

One of the greatest challenges the world is facing today is food insecurity. According to the United States Agency for International Development (USAID) the world has never faced a crisis like this present one. Nearly a billion people are food insecure, and there was a potential for the world to see another 265 million facing acute hunger by the end of the year 2020. Food insecurity has often been linked to poverty, however, the world pandemic—Covid-19—has exposed a new reality, namely that many of the "haves" are on the way to becoming the "have nots." In the United States, food pantry lines are becoming longer and longer. And it makes one wonder what is happening to the blessings of which people boasted concerning America.

The images of empty grocery store shelves, long lines at food banks, farmers dumping thousands of gallons of milk or plowing vegetables and other farm products into the ground because of the lock downs are all troubling. The scenes are sparking fears that we are about to lose the blessings of food—even in the United States, the country in which, to our shame, we dump more food than any other place in the world. As the virus spreads, we continue to see food distribution channels disrupted and panic buying adding to panic buying and hoarding. Food supplies are drying up, and millions of individuals are starving. What a contrast between our present reality and the story we are told of human origins, in which there was an abundance of provisions for the world!

Think of the divine command to humanity which says: "Of every tree of the garden you may freely eat" (Gen. 2:16, NKJV). What must it have been like to live in the lush garden, roaming around and eating to their heart's satisfaction? God offered only one prohibition, "But of the tree of the knowledge of good and evil you shall not eat, for in the day that you eat of it you shall surely die" (Gen. 2:17, NKJV). If the holy pair had not violated God's prohibition, they would constantly have had enough provisions and would not have been later told, "By the sweat of your brow you will eat your food until you return to the ground, since from it you were taken; for dust you are and to dust you will return" (Gen. 3:19, NIV). The violation of the prohibition not only created a problem for those in the garden, but it has been an inheritance through the generations. Even today we can see where the violations have led. Think of what has been done to make it so difficult to have abundant provisions today:

1. Over farming that has led to the depletion in the nutrients of many parts of the earth.
2. Overpopulation, where there are more people than can be fed.
3. Wars that destroy property.
4. Mass production through industrialization and mechanization.
5. Chemicals—poisoning the earth—helping to produce quickly but then less and less.
6. Climate change creates the melting of the ice caps from which water flows to water the land.
7. Slash and burn that have created soil erosion.
8. Hoarding by one part of the population.

We may debate whether humanity is responsible for all the soil erosion and fires that destroy the land or for the famines, however, the issue is whether we are appreciative enough of the provisions that God has given to us to take care of it.

Do we say "thanks" enough for all that He has provided for our well-being? Put in a simple question: How often do we see families sitting down to dinner today and thanking God for all that He has provided? The days when a family used to sit down and hold hands around a dinner table seem to have passed. In most dining rooms, a plaque used to hang, bearing the words:

Christ is the head of this house the unseen guest at every meal
The silent listener to every conversation.

Yes, signs in dining rooms recognizing the sense of appreciation for the provisions of which we partake have been taken down. They are gone. The change that has taken place seems to be predicated on the fact that the TV and other distractions are now so pervasive in our homes that they are taking our interests away from God. To this extent, we are forgetting to thank God for His provisions.

With this in mind, let us remind ourselves that, if we are able to sit down to eat, we are never to forget that we need to say a prayer of thankfulness to God for what we have and then pray for those who are in want. But we need to do more. We need to think of and find ways to share our morsels with others. In fact, let us think of the example of the four lepers at the gate of Samaria. A brief summary of the story in 2 Kings 3:7–20 is that it tells how Samaria was under siege from a Syrian army. Those inside the city were dying from thirst and starvation. The king therefore sent one of his servants to go inquire of the prophet Elisha what might happen. Were he and his people inside the city going to die? The prophet sent back a message with the servant that said, in summation, in twenty-four hours the economic situation in Samaria will be completely reversed. Instead of scarcity, there will be such abundance that food prices would radically drop in the city, the conditions of famine associated with the siege will cease.

What happened was just as Elisha prophesied. The next morning, the Lord caused the army of the Syrians to hear the noise of chariots and the noise of horses—as if it were the noise of a great army. So, the Syrians concluded that the king of Israel had hired the kings of the Hittites and the kings of the Egyptians to attack them, and they rose up and fled at dawn. They left the camp intact with their tents, their horses, their donkeys, and all their provisions.

The most interesting part of the story concerns how they learned of the abandonment of the camp. There were four lepers who were isolated away from the city. Sensing that they were about to die from starvation, they decided to go to the camp of the Syrians. The worst that could happen to them, they thought, was that the Syrians could take them prisoners. On reaching the camp, the lepers found that the Syrian army had deserted their camp, leaving all their provisions behind. Read the words of the narrator as he tells what happened next:

"And when these lepers came to the outskirts of the camp, they went into one tent and ate and drank, and carried from it silver and gold and clothing, and went and hid them; then they came back and entered another tent, and carried some from there also, and went and hid it. Then they said to one another, 'We are not doing right. This day is a day of good news, and we remain silent. If we wait until morning light, some punishment will come upon us. Now therefore, come, let us go and tell the king's household" (2 Kings 7:8, 9, NKJV, emphasis mine).

By sharing what they found with the gatekeepers of the city, the lepers were able to save the city dwellers from starvation.

The key point of reference in the story is to remind us that every time we sit down to a meal, we are to think of those about us who are facing food insecurity. Not only are we to think of those who are in the food lines, but we are to think of the many more who are facing starvation.

We are not only blessed when we can eat, but we are also blessed to share. Sharing a meal is one of the greatest privileges that God has given us. In fact, eating is a social activity. Anthropologists have recognized its importance. "Food is almost always shared; people eat together; mealtimes are events when the whole family or settlement or village comes together.... And because eating is almost always a group event (as opposed to sex), food becomes a focus of symbolic activity about sociality and our place in our society" (Robin Fox, "Food and Eating: An Anthological Perspective").

Yes, we need to say often how delightful the copious provisions are that God has given to us. We eat and drink:

1. To bring energy into our bodies
2. To build body strength
3. To create the right mood

4. To reduce all kinds of diseases
6. To improve our memory
7. To build longevity
8. To build self-esteem
9. To build our faith, in what God can do.

When we are tempted to distrust the power of God to provide, we need to think of the multiple stories in the Bible that tell how God provided. Think of the story of the manna and of the quails in the wilderness (Exod. 16). Think of how God allowed water to flow from a rock. Think of how God turned bitter water sweet (Exod. 15:23–26; 2 Kings 2:19). Think of the woman with the barrel of oil (2 Kings 4). Think of the woman with the flour (1 Kings 17). Think of how Jesus turned water into wine (John 4). Think of the feeding of the 5000 (Matt. 14:15–21) and the feeding of the 4000 (Matt. 15:32–39). The point is that despite the present conditions of our world, we need to appreciate the provisions that God has given us, and we need to think of those about us that are less fortunate and share the blessings of life with them.

Remember the words of the apostle Paul when you face distressing times, "My God shall supply all your need according to his riches in glory by Christ Jesus" (Phil. 4:19, KJV).

Take a Moment

When last have you stopped to thank God for the provisions that He has given to you instead of complaining of what you do not have?

_____
_____
_____
_____
_____

Write down a special provision that you would wish to ask the Lord to give you.

_____
_____
_____
_____
_____

Then, write down how and with whom you would wish to share the provision.

_____
_____
_____
_____
_____

The Blessings of Obedience

And the LORD God commanded the man, saying, "Of every tree of the garden you may freely eat; but of the tree of the knowledge of good and evil you shall not eat, for in the day that you eat of it you shall surely die." (Gen. 2:16, 17, NKJV)

> The key to receiving the blessings of God is to follow what God commands. Obedience is what was expected of the first couple on the earth, and obedience is what is expected for every generation of humanity. No one who is unwilling to obey should expect to enjoy the blessings of God. Blessings are predicated on obedience.

9.

The Blessings of Obedience

In the world in which we live today, "obedience" is often seen as a bad word. The exception is what parents expect from their children, or, in a more mundane way, what dog trainers expect of their dogs. And yet, from the beginning of time, it has been clear that, if humanity wants to live in the most wholesome way, all must follow the way of obedience. In effect, obedience is not an option; it is a requirement for a blessed life.

From the perspective of my reflection, God did not just create humanity and toss them into their garden environment and say, "Survive if you might." No, God gave humanity consciences to decide between right and wrong, minds to think, ears to listen to His voice, hearts to commune with Him, and commandments that we might obey Him.

Just think of it—if Eve had only listened to what God said to her and had not talked to the serpent, who tempted her to disobey what God had said, she would have remained on the path of obedience. A great spiritual writer has told us: "Nothing short of obedience can be accepted" (*The Desire of Ages*, p. 523). Thus, if Eve had been obedient, her blessings would not have turned into curses. Let's reflect on Eve's actions.

> Now the serpent was more cunning than any beast of the field which the LORD God had made. And he said to the woman, "Has God indeed said, 'You shall not eat of every tree of the garden'? And the woman said to the serpent, "We may eat the fruit of the trees of the garden; but of the fruit of the tree which is in the midst of the garden, God has said, 'You shall not eat it, nor shall you touch it, lest you die.' " Then the serpent said to the woman, "You will not surely die. For God knows that in the day you eat of it your eyes will be opened, and you will be like God, knowing good and evil." So, when the woman saw that the tree was good for food, that it was pleasant to the eyes, and a tree desirable to make one wise, she took of its fruit and ate. She also gave to her husband with her, and he ate (Gen. 3:1–6, NKJV).

It is also clear that Adam was no better than Eve. He knew God's requirement, yet he listened to Eve and followed her suggestion, and his disobedience brought death upon all humanity. In fact, Adam is identified as the one with the greater responsibility of disobedience because, in the creation order, he came first and was given the responsibility to be the head steward of the earth (Gen. 2:5–25). This is why Scripture says that, through the disobedience of one man (which was Adam), death came into the world and death by sin (Rom. 5:12), and, "through the disobedience of the one man [that is, Adam] the many were made sinners" (Rom. 5:19). Like it or not, humanity has to admit that something has gone wrong in the creation. Our disobedience has brought multiple curses in place of the blessings that God promised in His original plan. I wish we could reflect further on the consequences of disobedience here, but the purpose of this reflection is to note what it means to follow the way of obedience and enjoy the heavenly blessings.

The principal thought that comes to mind from the statement above is that, to receive the blessings of obedience, we must make sure that we know to whom we are listening, that we are following the right voice, the precise rules, and the correct commands. In the time of the coronavirus, we are instructed simply to:

1. Wash our hands (for 20 seconds at least).
2. Use the right sanitizers to clean our hands often.
3. Wear masks—the right kind of masks.
4. Self-quarantine (if you feel sick).
5. Practice social distancing—keeping at least six feet from other people in public spaces.
6. Gather only in small groups (some places, no more than five or ten people).
7. Stay away from a sugary diet and other things that will compromise our immune system.
8. Get enough rest at night.
9. Get sunlight and fresh air.
10. Get tested if you feel your body has been compromised.
11. Take the necessary precautions recommended for your protection.
12. You cannot be careless and expect to be covered.

These guidelines are straightforward. Yet, because people have shied away from following the orders as given by the CDC, FDA, surgeon general, and other reliable medical practitioners, the world is suffering some of the most tragic negative consequences.

The point is that disobedience has awful consequences. So, we need to make clear the voices to which we are listening and obey the right ones. Know from whom we are taking orders. Be clear on what our orders are. When we hear: Touch not; taste not; look not; walk not; make not; think not; fear not, we need to ask who is speaking, and if it is right, we need to obey. When we hear the command to look "unto Jesus the author and finisher of your faith" (Heb. 12:2, KJV) or to "remember now your Creator in the days of your youth, before the difficult days come, and the years draw near when you say, 'I have no pleasure in them' " (Eccles. 12:1, NKJV), we do not have to guess what our response needs to be. All we need to say is what the child Samuel was to say, "Speak, LORD, for your servant is listening" (1 Sam. 3:9, NIV).

> *To receive the blessings of obedience, we must make sure that we know to whom we are listening, that we are following the right voice, the precise rules, and the correct commands.*

Of course, there is negative obedience that we ought to avoid. We are cautioned not to listen to the instructions that have no real value for our existence. There are those who suggest that they are "just following orders." But we need to remind them that human beings are not robots. We all have choices and can make responsible decisions. Responsible decisions allow us to be healthy and guilt-free and to keep our relationship with the divine. In maintaining that relationship, we will avoid distractions, deviation, and, therefore, destruction. Only when we stay on the path of positive obedience will we share in the blessings of God.

I have been thinking through the blessings and have listed here thirty blessings that are given to us as a result of our positive obedience:

1. Enjoyment of full fellowship with God (Gen. 6:8; 1 Sam. 7:10–12).
2. Positive influence on others—the blessings benefit us, and they benefit others (Deut. 5:29, 33; 6:3; Ps. 119:95, 96; Jer. 7:23).
3. Joy and peace will be brought to our souls (Jer. 6:16; 33:8, 9).
4. God will be a Father to us (Gen. 17:7; Exod. 6:7; Ezek. 34:24; 36:28; 2 Cor. 6:16).

5. We shall be sons and daughters of God (2 Cor. 6:18).
6. The welfare of our children will be made secure in God (Ps. 102:28).
7. We will receive help from God (Zech. 4:6; Phil. 2:13).
8. We will be sanctified by God (Rom. 6:22; 2 Cor. 7:1).
9. Our lives will be preserved by God (Prov. 30:5; John 12:25).
10. Our lives will be protected from danger (Gen. 7:6–11; Ps. 34:7).
11. Our lives will be restored into balance by God (Ps. 19:11).
12. The guilt and shame of our lives will be transformed (Ps. 19:7, 8).
13. We will secure prosperity promised us by God (1 Kings 2:3; Joshua 1:8).
14. Our plans will be established in God (Prov. 16:3).
15. We will receive promotions that will surprise us by the help of the divine (Ps. 75:6, 7).
16. We will develop more disciplined characters in God (Prov. 1:8, 9).
17. We will have wisdom from God–that is, a more understanding heart (Prov. 19:13; 1 Kings 3:1–14).
18. We will receive the forgiveness of God and the ability to pardon others (Matt. 6:12; 18:35).
19. We will enjoy freedom in Christ (Rom. 6:16–19).
20. Our faith will develop (1 John 2:3–6).
21. We will inherit the good of the land—even an earthly inheritance (Isa. 1:19).
22. We will receive strength to meet the complex challenges of any moment (Joshua 24:15).
23. We will be drawing closer to God, becoming a friend of God (John 14:21).
24. We will be used in more effective ways by God (Gen. 12, Exod. 3, Luke 1).
25. We will get to the divine destiny (Hab. 2:3).
26. God will become our defender (Exod. 22:23).
27. We will fulfill one of the conditions to the answers to our prayers (Prov. 28:9; 1 John 3:22).
28. We will have the possibility of longer life in the earth (Exod. 20:12; Eph. 6:1–3).
29. We will receive the right of eternal life (Rev. 21:8; 2 Cor. 5:10).
30. We will have the right to enter into the gates into the Eternal City (Rev. 2:7; 22:2, 14, 19).

God has spoken. He has been very clear that our blessings are conditioned upon our obedience. Can we fail to obey Him? Maybe you have sung the hymn, "Trust and Obey," and do not know its backstory, but it is of interest. The story is that it was written following an incident that took place at one of Dwight L. Moody's revival meetings in 1887. A young man who had just given his life to the Lord Jesus Christ was reportedly heard saying, "I am not quite sure—I am going to trust and obey." One of those listening to him was the music director of the Moody Bible Institute, Professor Towner. Based on the young man's comment, Professor Towner, with the help of John Sammis, who developed the lyrics, composed the music to the hymn, "Trust and Obey," which is also known as, "When we walk with the Lord." The words truly express the feelings of many individuals who are asked to obey Christ. To each of these we can say that no one can obey on their own, but we can all obey if we receive the help of God. Like the apostle Paul says: "I can do all things through Christ who strengthens me" (Phil. 4:13, NKJV).

Take a Moment

Write down any blessing that the above reading has brought to your mind today and for which you would wish to thank the Lord.

_____
_____
_____
_____
_____

Further, write down a special blessing that you would wish to ask the Lord to give you.

_____
_____
_____
_____
_____

Then, write down how and with whom you would wish to share your blessing.

_____
_____
_____
_____
_____

The Blessings of Salvation

"And I will put enmity between you and the woman, and between your seed and her Seed; He shall bruise your head, and you shall bruise His heel." (Gen. 3:15, NKJV)

> "The blessings of our salvation are incalculably great, and the proper response is to bless God for the riches he has bestowed upon us in Christ." (Brandon Crowe, *The Message of the General Epistles in the History of Redemption*, p. 14)

10.

The Blessings of Salvation

It is of interest to me how people who argue that life in this world came into existence through an evolutionary process do not accept the reality of the Fall or the plan of salvation. Contrarily, the Bible that acknowledges the Fall, also teaches the necessity of salvation. But it must be noted that the consequences of the Fall bring a curse. Two times in the story of the Fall, as stated in Genesis 3, there are explicit mentions of the curse (Gen. 3:14, 17):

a. There was a curse on the serpent.
b. There was a curse on the ground.

Although there was no eternal curse on Adam and Eve, yet neither did they get off scot-free. They faced the harsh reality of their failures, which included death. No, they did not get off, and they were able to see the curses that came on the earth and on their progeny, directly and indirectly. By the time the curses were pronounced on the serpent and on the ground, Adam and Eve had already sensed the consequence of death, as was foretold by God, when the pair was being instructed how to steward the earth. God said, "But you must not eat from the tree of the knowledge of good and evil, for when you eat from it you will certainly die" (Gen. 2:17, NIV). Yes, as soon as they fell, they sensed the first haunt of death. Among the other penalties included their perception of "nakedness." Their eyes were opened, and they saw that they were "naked." That is, they lost their innocence in multiple ways. They felt guilty, sorrowful, fearful, and depressed. What would have been an experience of joyful ecstasy God predicted to be an experience with contradiction. Here are His pronouncements to Eve and then to Adam:

"I will make your pains in childbearing very severe; with painful labor you will give birth to children. Your desire will be for your husband, and he will rule over you" (Gen. 3:16, NIV).

"Because you have listened to the voice of your wife and have eaten from the tree of which I commanded you not to eat, cursed is the ground because of you; through toil you will eat of it all the days of your life" (Gen. 3:17, Berean Study Bible).

These were hard to hear, but such were the consequences of disobedience. Before giving the curses, God had pronounced His blessings. Here is how it was stated:

> And I will put enmity
> Between you and the woman,
> And between your seed and her Seed;
> He shall bruise your head,
> And you shall bruise His heel. (Gen. 3:15, NKJV)

This was the greatest prophecy of all times. It is called by many theologians the protoevangelium, or "first gospel"—the good news that God was going to do something about the situation of misery into which humanity had placed itself. In this passage of just 28 words, one can see essentially five clauses, which are five lines of poetry. But it is the most powerful announcement that could have ever been repeated to the bewildered pair and to all their progeny. A "Seed" would come through the woman, and between the Seed and the serpent there would be enmity.

The serpent would constantly seek to hurt the Seed of the woman, but the Seed would overcome. Also, the serpent would hurt the heel of the woman, but the serpent would be overcome.

Yes, the story of the struggle between the serpent and the Seed of the woman is remarkable, as it makes clear the cost to bring about the salvation of humankind, the correction of the sin problem, the reversal of the deception that led to their sin, and the removal of the deceiver who offered the deception that led to their sin.

In a variety of ways, the Promised Seed became the hope for every generation of humanity, though the prophecy about His coming was not always understood. Adam and Eve did not grasp it clearly, for, when Cain was born as their first child, they thought that he would be the Promised Seed. Genesis tells us: "Now Adam knew Eve his wife, and she conceived and bore Cain, and said, 'I have acquired a man from the LORD' " (Gen. 4:1, NKJV). It might seem rather mild to us that Eve would name her firstborn a name that means "acquired," or "gotten." But there was more to it than that. A particularly important part in the story is the giveaway when Eve took note that she was "given" a child "from the Lord." She assumed, in naming him Cain, that he would be the Seed that would remove their curse. *This first child is the Seed*, she thought. He would be the one to undo the curse and bring the blessing. But Cain turned out to be a murderer, and, after he killed

> *The effort to fulfill His mission cost the Seed His life.*

his brother, he became a vagabond. Eve's hopes were dashed, at least for a while, until she had a third son, Seth, who likewise was not the Seed, but Seth became the covenant line from which the Seed would be born.

After thousands of years, the Seed did come. Abraham at first thought that it was his servant Eliezer (Gen. 15:1, 2). He also thought it was in his first son Ishmael, but neither of these was the one that God intended. Then he thought, along with his wife Sarah, that Isaac was the Seed, but he was not. It took an estimated 2000 years from the time of Abraham until the Seed came in the person of Jesus Christ. By that time, the interpretation of the promise was so corrupted that many rejected the Seed out of hand (John 1:11). However, what God told Eve was perfectly fulfilled. The promised Seed was planted in the womb of Mary. His name was "Jesus" because, as the angel explained to Joseph, He was to save His people from their sins (Matt. 1:21). Jesus later announced this as His priority, "For the Son of Man is come to seek and to save that which was lost" (Luke 19:10, NKJV). The effort to fulfill His mission cost the Seed His life. When He died on the cross, the serpent thought that He had thwarted the mission, but, on the morning of the resurrection, it became clear that the Seed had achieved total victory. The Seed came forth from the grave a victor. He had secured the salvation of humankind. In ecstatic tones, Paul reflects, in Romans 5, the Seed's accomplishments. They boil down to 17 blessings:

1. We have peace with God.
2. We have access to the throne of grace and mercy.
3. We stand before the throne in grace.
4. We have freedom from guilt.
5. We have freedom from shame.
6. We have freedom from fear.
7. We have joy in the midst of our suffering.
8. We have the gift of salvation.
9. We have hope that things will be better than they now are.
10. We have eternal life.

11. We have come to know the love of God.
12. We have assurance and security.
13. We have help for our helpless situation.
14. We have strength to face persecution.
15. We have propitiation for our sin.
16. We have the righteousness of God.
17. We have the forgiveness of our sins.

These seventeen blessings are a bare minimum of the enormous number of blessings that Christ has provided for us. In Ephesians 1:3–20, the apostle Paul focuses on another fifteen spiritual blessings that are offered to us in the heavenly realm. And we have these blessings because we are in Christ. We are not taking time to list them here, but I mention them because they have profound significance, and I encourage you to make yourself available to receive them.

Today, Christ is in the heavenly places of the heavenly sanctuary, completing His work of intercession so that one day He can hand out His final blessing, when He will say:

> "Come, you who are blessed by my Father; take your inheritance, the kingdom prepared for you since the creation of the world." (Matt. 25:34, NIV)

Take a Moment

Write down the blessing that the above reading has brought to your mind today and for which you would wish to thank the Lord.

_____
_____
_____
_____
_____
_____

Further, write down a special blessing that you would wish to ask the Lord to give you.

_____
_____
_____
_____
_____
_____

Then, write down how and with whom you would wish to share your blessing.

_____
_____
_____
_____
_____
_____

The Blessings Redirected

This is the book of the genealogy of Adam. In the day that God created man, He made him in the likeness of God. He created them male and female, and blessed them and called them Mankind in the day they were created. And Adam lived one hundred and thirty years, and begot a son in his likeness, after his image, and named him Seth. After he begot Seth, the days of Adam were eight hundred years; and he had sons and daughters. So all the days that Adam lived were nine hundred and thirty years; and he died. (Gen. 5:1–5)

> The Bible provides us with multiple examples of what God is ever seeking to do to redirect the course of history. When humanity goes off course, God constantly finds a way to re-establish His covenant of blessing.

11.

The Blessings Redirected

Every time I read Genesis 5:1–5, I am intrigued by the effort that God makes to redirect the course of history for blessings. When humanity makes a mess of history, God intervenes and rewrites the story. What follows shows His redirecting from earth's earliest history.

> And Adam lived one hundred and thirty years, and begot a son in his own likeness, after his image, and named him Seth. After he begot Seth, the days of Adam were eight hundred years; and he had sons and daughters. So all the days that Adam lived were nine hundred and thirty years; and he died. (Gen. 5:3–5, NKJV)

The story is not about the age of Adam. It is about the graciousness of God. It is about what God was doing to rewrite the story in the earliest history of humanity. After God poured His original blessings on Adam and Eve, they fell into sin, and the history of humanity took a new trajectory. Soon Cain, the first son of Adam and Eve, killed Abel, their second son, and his arrogance led to his separation from God. He became a wanderer who raised up an idolatrous generation.

In loving kindness, God sought to redirect the course of history by finding a person who would be true to God's covenant. He therefore gave Adam and Eve a son by the name of Seth. In commenting on the birth of Seth, Ellen White wrote:

> To Adam was given another son to be the heir of the spiritual birthright. The name Seth, given to this son, signified "appointed," or "compensation"; "for," said the mother, "God hath appointed me another seed instead of Abel, whom Cain slew." Seth resembled Adam more closely than did his other sons, a worthy character following in the steps of Abel. Yet he inherited no more natural goodness than did Cain. Seth, like Cain, inherited the fallen nature of his parents. But he received also the knowledge of the Redeemer and instruction

in righteousness. He labored, as Abel would have done, to turn the minds of sinful men to revere and obey their Creator. (Ellen G. White, *From Eternity Past*, p. 43)

It is a fact of interest that, when Seth had his first son, he named him Enosh. What a name to give a son! According to Strong's Concordance and other lexicographers and commentators, the name means "man," "mortal," "weak," or "sick." However, the commentator I referenced in the paragraph above says that Seth taught his son the way of the Lord. The striking biblical phrase connected with the birth of Enosh states that "at that time people began to call upon the name of the Lord" (Gen. 4:26, ESV). Commentators have a variety of interpretations of what the phrase means, but the most consistent view is that those in the lineage of Seth were carrying forward the great effort of reform to get away from the idolatrous children of Cain. After killing his brother Abel, Cain felt responsible for himself. He thought he could build his own security by taking his destiny into his own hands. It is said that:

1. Cain stands at the head of the class of human beings that worship the gods of this world.
2. Cain tried to make a new world, and it was not one that would be ruled by God.
3. Cain decided that God would be no more adequate for his life.

Therefore, God had to do all that He could to set a new beginning of history. In Seth, God found an agent to build His new covenant community. Seth was:

1. The replacement of Abel.
2. The representative head of the faithful.
3. The ancestor of the righteous in the antediluvian world.
4. The restarter of the new covenant line that had begun with Adam and continued through Enoch, Methuselah, and Lamech, the father of Noah.

Seth had a long life. The record says, "Seth lived one hundred and five years, and begot Enosh. After he begot Enosh, Seth lived eight hundred and seven years, and had sons and daughters. So all the days of Seth were nine hundred and twelve years; and he died" (Gen. 5:6–8, NKJV). Yes, Seth died. But the story of Seth did not end with his death. His influence continued for generations. Thus, it would be said of Enoch, the anchor of the sixth generation that followed Seth, "Enoch walked with God and he was not for God took him" (Gen. 5:24, NKJV). Later, it was said of Seth's grandson Noah, "Noah found grace in the eyes of the Lord" (Gen. 6:8, KJV). This is to place emphasis on the covenant generation.

The key observation is that, at times, God has to intervene, interrupt, and redirect history to bring His blessings to future generations.

Take a Moment

Write down any blessing that the above reading has brought to your mind today and for which you would wish to thank the Lord.

_____
_____
_____
_____
_____
_____

Further, write down a special blessing that you would wish to ask the Lord to give you.

_____
_____
_____
_____
_____
_____

Then, write down how and with whom you would wish to share your blessing.

_____
_____
_____
_____
_____
_____

The Blessings of Noah

So God blessed Noah and his sons, and said to them: "Be fruitful and multiply, and fill the earth. And the fear of you and the dread of you shall be on every beast of the earth, on every bird of the air, on all that move on the earth, and on all the fish of the sea. They are given into your hand. Every moving thing that lives shall be food for you. I have given you all things, even as the green herbs. But you shall not eat flesh with its life, that is, its blood." (Gen. 9:1–4, NKJV)

> The blessings that God gave Noah (Gen. 9:1-4) are the same as the original blessings that were offered to Adam at the beginning of the Creation (Gen. 1:22, 28) and that would later be offered to Abraham and to all who are willing to live according to the divine Covenant until the end of time (Gen. 12:1-3, 7, 8).

12.

The Blessings of Noah

After meditating on the words that are contained in Genesis 9:1–4, I was exultant with praise. They make me cry out, again, and again, "How merciful is God!" Yes, I have taken note that following the Flood, God re-pronounced special blessings on Noah and his three sons. The blessings followed the trajectory of blessings that had been pronounced upon Adam and his family from the beginning of the creation (see Gen. 1:27). In thinking of the post antediluvian rebellion, I cry out in the words of Jeremiah, "The steadfast love of God never ceases; his mercies never come to an end, they are new every morning, great is your faithfulness" (Lam. 3:22, 23, ESV). Despite the fact that God had to bring judgment through the Flood, God in His mercy preserved humanity through Noah and his family. What the Psalmist declared of that time is true today—God "will not always strive with us, nor will He keep His anger forever" (Ps. 103:9, NKJV). Yes, despite what we have done, God has done and continues to do everything that He can do to save us.

Of course, God does everything to save and bless us, regardless of our rebellion. Disobedience and rebellion brought the curse on the earth that led to the Flood. And any disobedience will bring its curse on the earth as well. We might observe that, after the Flood, curses were mixed in with the blessings. As part of God's blessings, Noah became a farmer. "And Noah began to be a husbandman, and he planted a vineyard: And he drank of the wine, and was drunken; and he was uncovered within his tent. And Ham, the father of Canaan, saw the nakedness of his father, and told his two brethren without. And Shem and Japheth took a garment, and laid it upon both their shoulders, and went backward, and covered the nakedness of their father; and their faces were backward, and they saw not their father's nakedness" (Gen. 9:20–23, KJV). "So Noah awoke from his wine, and knew what his younger son had done to him. Then he said: 'Cursed be Canaan; a servant of servants shall he be unto his brethren.' And he said,

'Blessed be the LORD, the God of Shem, and may Canaan be his servant" (Gen. 9:24–26, NKJV).

I won't go into the sardonic interpretations that have been promoted concerning the "Curse of Ham," since they have been debunked by so many who understand that such interpretations were constructed to support the enslavement of Africans, Canaanites, or other peoples. There is no place for such absurdity. It is of interest that, regardless of the blessings on Shem and Japheth, their children were, at points, enslaved by the children of Ham. Those today who think they have a right to put people down and enslave them, in one way, or another need to recognize that they are not carrying God's blessing (see Gen. 15:14; Isa. 13:11).

The blessing pronounced on Noah was passed on through his sons. That is why we read that Noah proclaimed: "May God enlarge Japheth, and may he dwell in the tents of Shem; and may Canaan be his servant" (Gen. 9:27, NKJV).

There is a sharp contrast between the attitude of God and that of Noah. God blessed Noah and his sons. But, after Noah got drunk, he cursed Cainan, not taking responsibility for his own actions. In his anger and embarrassment, he cursed his grandson Canaan because Noah's son Ham saw his father naked and laughed. Other than that, what Ham did is not clear. Is it that Ham just saw his father's nakedness and made mockery of him, calling his two brothers to come to look at him? Did he commit some act of immorality as is suggested by some commentators? No one is sure, but the point is that Ham's disrespect caused Noah to curse Ham's son.

Noah's actions have led me to wonder whether I have always acted responsibly before my children? Have they been cursed by any of my foolish actions? Have I passed curses onto them and onto my grandchildren insomuch that the curses have become generational?

My reflections are not to place guilt on myself or anyone else. However, I have seen too many parents who, after returning to God, turn upon their children to blame and curse their negative behaviors. Instead of penitential petitions for their children, they have blamed and shamed their children. One member of a church I pastored, who often criticized the young people's dress and behavior, had been a lapsed prodigal for years in the world. So now that person wanted to make everybody perfect.

It is good that God is so merciful to each of us. If, by any means, God would treat us as we deserve, we would all be living under the curse of

Cainan. Think of the blessings that Noah received from the Lord, and which he was allowed to pass onto the generations beyond.

1. Noah found grace in the eyes of the Lord.
2. Then God spoke to Noah about building an ark.
3. God told Noah to go into the ark.
4. God shut the door of the ark to save Noah.
5. God protected Noah in the ark during the Flood.
6. God sent an angel to open the door of the ark so that Noah and his family could enter in.
7. God put a rainbow in the sky as a covenant of promise, saying He would never again destroy the earth by a flood.
8. God put the fear of Noah on all the animals of the earth.
9. God provided food for Noah and his family after the Flood.
10. God allowed a violent wind to dry up the waters of the Flood and to cover the bodies of the dead creatures.
11. God allowed Noah the privilege of blessing his sons, Shem and Japheth.
12. God pardoned Noah of his sin of drunkenness, even though by his drunkenness he had made a fool of himself.

We have been told that after leaving the ark, Noah did not forget to bless God for being preserved. His first act after leaving the ark "was to build an altar and offer a sacrifice, thus manifesting his gratitude to God for deliverance and his faith in Christ, the great sacrifice. This offering was pleasing to the Lord, and a blessing" not only on him but on his family and on all who should live upon the earth (Ellen G. White, *From Eternity Past*, pp. 61, 62).

Every time we look at a rainbow, we are to remind ourselves of the blessings that were given to Noah and to us.

Every time we look at a rainbow, we are to remind ourselves of the blessings that were given to Noah and to us. In fact, while curses are said to last "unto the third and to the fourth generation" (Exod. 34:7, KJV), blessings are "perpetual" (Gen. 9:12, KJV) to "a thousand generations" (Exod. 20:6, NIV).

Take a Moment

Write down the blessing that the above reading has brought to your mind today and for which you would wish to thank the Lord.

_____
_____
_____
_____
_____
_____

Further, write down a special blessing that you would wish to ask the Lord to give you.

_____
_____
_____
_____
_____
_____

Then, write down how and with whom you would wish to share your blessing.

_____
_____
_____
_____
_____
_____

The Blessings of Abraham

I will make you a great nation; I will bless you and make your name great; and you shall be a blessing. I will bless those who bless you, and I will curse him who curses you; and in you all the families of the earth shall be blessed. (Gen. 12:2, 3, NKJV)

> The blessings of Abraham are illustrative of how God's blessings flow. God gave Abraham blessings—not to hoard them but to share them with all about him and with the generations that would follow him. As it is said, "If you belong to Christ you are Abraham's seed and heirs of the promise" (Gal. 3:29).

13.

The Blessings of Abraham

It is of interest how, at times, God calls us away from our places of comfort to bless us. The story of Abraham is very typical—no, we might say, it is archetypical. He was the first in the biblical record to be removed from his country, family, friends, and neighborhoods to be blessed as he was. God blessed him, and he, in turn, was to be a channel of blessing to all nations of the earth. We find the introduction to his story in Genesis 12, which states:

> Now the LORD had said to Abram: "Get out of your country, from your family and from your father's house, to a land that I will show you." (Gen. 12:1, NKJV)

Yes, God took Abraham from his comfort zone because God saw him to be someone distinctive from those in his community. God was looking for a man with whom He could talk and who would listen to Him, one who would be a friend of God, who would be willing to obey Him, and who would be loyal and faithful to Him. God saw that He could accomplish His purpose through Abraham.

Abraham's home in Ur of the Chaldees, today's Iraq, was an idolatrous place, and, if Abraham had remained there, he would have been corrupted by the system. Therefore, God called him out so that He could be gracious to him. The call was particular to Abraham, but he was not called by himself, rather, he represented a channel of grace to all who would have faith in God. His call meant the universalizing of the gospel.

Yes, Abraham was blessed and became an instrument of blessing to the world. God had to remove him from his comfortable zone as He had to remove the nation of Israel from the land of promise and send them among the other nations, so that they could spread the blessings received. Here is how the covenant blessings were outlined to Abraham:

1. "I will make you a great nation;
2. I will bless you

3. And make your name great;
4. And you shall be a blessing.
5. I will bless those who bless you,
6. And I will curse him who curses you;
7. And in you all the families of the earth shall be blessed" (Gen. 12:2, 3, NKJV).

The enumeration of the blessings outlined above are notable. But, again, such blessings did not come to Abraham, regardless of how he had lived. What is clearly stated is that Abraham was—

1. A disciplined father. This is why God said of him, "For I have chosen him, so that he will direct his children and his household after him to keep the way of the LORD by doing what is right and just, so that the LORD will bring about for Abraham what he has promised him" (Gen. 18:19, NIV).
2. A man with extraordinary faith. This is why the apostle Paul wrote: "Abraham believed God, and it was credited to him as righteousness" (Rom. 4:3, NIV).
3. A very obedient man. When called of God, he did not resist. He was ready to move. This is why we read in Genesis 12: "So Abram departed as the LORD had spoken to him, and Lot went with him. And Abram was seventy-five years old when he departed from Haran" (Gen. 12:4, NKJV).

Abraham was not perfect. At least two times on recorded, when he feared for his life and was seeking to protect Sarah, he lied. He lost faith. He told Sarah to say she was his sister. Factually, Sarah was his half-sister. But half-truths are not the whole truth. As the story was told, it was a half-truth and thus a lie. It is thus of interest how, on each occasion, God intervened by stopping the king of Egypt and then the king of Gerar from violating Sarah. Further, the kings rebuked Abraham. (Read the full stories in Genesis, chapters 12 and 20.) Thus, God intervened to transform the situation. (See Ellen G. White, *Patriarchs and Prophets*, p. 130.)

If there was any blessing in the situations, it is that God stepped in to rescue His own name, His own reputation. Thus, the God of Abraham was made known to the kings and their nations. The wealth of Abraham also increased, as he received an offering of penitence from each king. The story points to the fact that, at times when under pressure, a child of God may manifest weaknesses, but God will use their situation to be a blessing. The apostle Paul says concerning the weakness of his physical condition, though it is applicable here, "for when I am weak, then am I strong" (2 Cor. 12:10, KJV). And then he wrote later, "And we know that all things work together for good to those who love God, to those who are the called according to His purpose" (Rom. 8:28, NKJV). What we learn from the blessing of Abraham, on the two occasions we have referenced, is that God's blessings are not dependent on any human merit but upon divine favor.

We might also point to the fact that, with all the blessing he received, Abraham also had to learn patience. After he and Sarah had waited some ten or eleven years from the promise of receiving an heir, Sarah got impatient and encouraged Abraham to take Hagar for a wife, and she bore Ishmael. The home of Abraham then became a place of conflict and misery (Gen. 16; 17). But, again, God worked with Abraham, so that, fourteen years later, his heir Isaac was born. By then Abraham had matured in faith and patience insomuch that God asked him to sacrifice Isaac (Gen. 22:1–19). The request to sacrifice Isaac was a test of Abraham's (1) faith, (2) love, and (3) obedience. Here, Abraham passed the test, and that is why the Lord stopped him as he raised the knife to take the life of Isaac, declaring: "Now I know that you fear God" (Gen. 22:12, NKJV).

Abraham is called "the father of the faithful," not because he was perfect but because he trusted himself wholly to God. He became the head of the covenant lineage that brought forth Jesus, the Seed of promise, through whom all the blessings of heaven flow, not only to those of the bloodline of Israel but also to those of the faith-line of Israel—to believing Jews and Gentiles alike. As the apostle Paul says in Romans:

> Therefore it is of faith that it might be according to grace, so that the promise might be sure to all the seed, not only to those who are of the law, but also to those who are of the faith of Abraham, who is the father of us all. (Rom. 4:16, NKJV)

When we step out in faith, it means that we are trusting God fully with whatever comes next. Watch Abraham and see how his faith grew—from trembling faith to trusting faith.

Take a Moment

Write down the blessing that the above reading has brought to your mind today and for which you would wish to thank the Lord.

_____
_____
_____
_____
_____

Further, write down a special blessing that you would wish to ask the Lord to give you.

_____
_____
_____
_____
_____

Then, write down how and with whom you would wish to share your blessing.

_____
_____
_____
_____
_____

The Blessings from Melchizedek

"Blessed be Abram of God Most High, Possessor of heaven and earth; And blessed be God Most High, who has delivered your enemies into your hand." And he gave him a tithe of all. (Gen. 14:19, 20, NKJV)

> When you gain a victory over the enemy, bless the Lord. Say with the Psalmist, "Bless the Lord, O my soul: and all that is within me, bless his holy name. Bless the Lord, O my soul, and forget not all his benefits" (Ps. 103:1, 2, KJV).

14.

The Blessings from Melchizedek

It is a great thing when those about us can recognize that God has blessed us. I do not just mean materially but emotionally, relationally, spiritually, and in other ways. This was evident in the meeting between Melchizedek and Abraham. The story is told in Genesis 14 about how the four kings of Shinar, namely, Amraphael, Arioch of Ellazar, Chedorlaomer of Elam, and Tidal of Goyim (or "nations"), formed a coalition to war against the king of Sodom and four other kings in the Valley of Siddim. Amraphael and his cohort won the war and drove away with the spoils of Sodom. But in their victory celebration, the kings made one mistake, they took hostages, including Lot, the nephew of Abraham. When Abraham learned that Lot was taken, he gathered a little band of 300 of his household and went out to fight the four kings of Shinar. It was quite shocking for everyone around when Abraham was able to overcome the cohort, bring back Lot and the other hostages, as well as the goods that were taken from Sodom. On his way from the rescue, Abraham met Melchizedek, the king of Salem (later called "Jerusalem"). In recognition of Abraham's victory, Melchizedek joined Abraham in a communion celebration to God. The story says that, "Melchizedek the king of Salem brought out bread and wine" to share with Abraham. Then "he blessed him and said: 'Blessed be Abram of God Most High, Possessor of heaven and earth; and blessed be God Most High, who has delivered your enemies into your hand.' And he gave him a tithe of all" (Gen. 14:19, 20, NKJV).

A key point in the story is that Melchizedek mysteriously appeared from nowhere to bless Abraham. That is how blessings arrive. They often come as surprises, and, as some might say, from "nowhere." The blessing Melchizedek offered was not of his own making but was from "God Most High," the only true source of blessings. The encounter between Melchizedek and Abraham teaches many lessons.

1. It affirmed that Abraham was truly a servant of the Most High God.

2. It confirmed that Abraham was on a true faith journey.
3. It gave recognition that the hand of God was working behind the scenes to lead Abraham to a successful arrival at his destination.
4. It was a prophecy that God would be with Abraham and his progeny in their covenant experiences.
5. It says there are qualities in a blessing that money cannot buy.
6. It contrasts two realities, namely, that of the God of peace and the city of Salem, which is the city of peace, later to be called Jerusalem. Jerusalem stood in contrast to Shinar, which is Babel, the city of confusion and the city of war. Jerusalem would be symbolic, not just in an earthly historical sense, but the Jerusalem of God would come from above.
7. It says God has in store millions of blessings for His faithful ones, who will be faithful through time and eternity.

The blessing of Melchizedek upon Abraham also shows that, when God blesses His children, the world will take notice. As noted, the kings of Egypt and the king of Gerar took notice that Abraham was blessed. Peoples of other nations took notice, even as the generations that followed Abraham were blessed. Many coveted the blessings. But they came to learn that those whom God blesses no one can curse. Take note of the effort of Balak, the king of Moab, who invited Balaam to curse Israel. How did it turn out? Each attempt at cursing turned into blessings. (Read Numbers 22–25.) The Apostle Paul says that we are letters of recommendation, written in the heart, known and read by all human beings (2 Cor. 3:2). The prophet Isaiah says, "Their descendants will be recognized and honored among the nations. Everyone will realize that they are a people the LORD has blessed" (Isa. 61:9, NLT).

Yes, when a person is blessed of God, it will show. It showed on Joseph. It showed on Daniel. And there is no question that it will show on us who love God the same as they did.

> *Can the world see Jesus in me?*
> *Can the world see Jesus in you? Does your love to Him ring true,*
> *And your life and service, too?*
> *Can the world see Jesus in you?*

These questions, asked by song writer Leila Morris, are appropriate, but let me ask the same thing another way:

1. Have you encountered any servant of God who has brought you a blessing?
2. Has anyone told you that you are blessed?
3. Has anyone told you that you have been a blessing to them?

Blessings received will show. People might not like it, but they will see it.

Take a Moment

Write down the blessing that the above reading has brought to your mind today and for which you would wish to thank the Lord.

_____
_____
_____
_____
_____
_____

Further, write down a special blessing that you would wish to ask the Lord to give you.

_____
_____
_____
_____
_____
_____

Then, write down how and with whom you would wish to share your blessing.

_____
_____
_____
_____
_____
_____

The Blessings of Tithing

"And praise be to God Most High, who delivered your enemies into your hand." Then Abram gave him a tenth of everything. (Gen. 14:20, NIV)

> Abraham returned a tithe and received a blessing. He took his tithe off the top of the spoils. He was showing his gratitude, faith, love, and obedience to God.

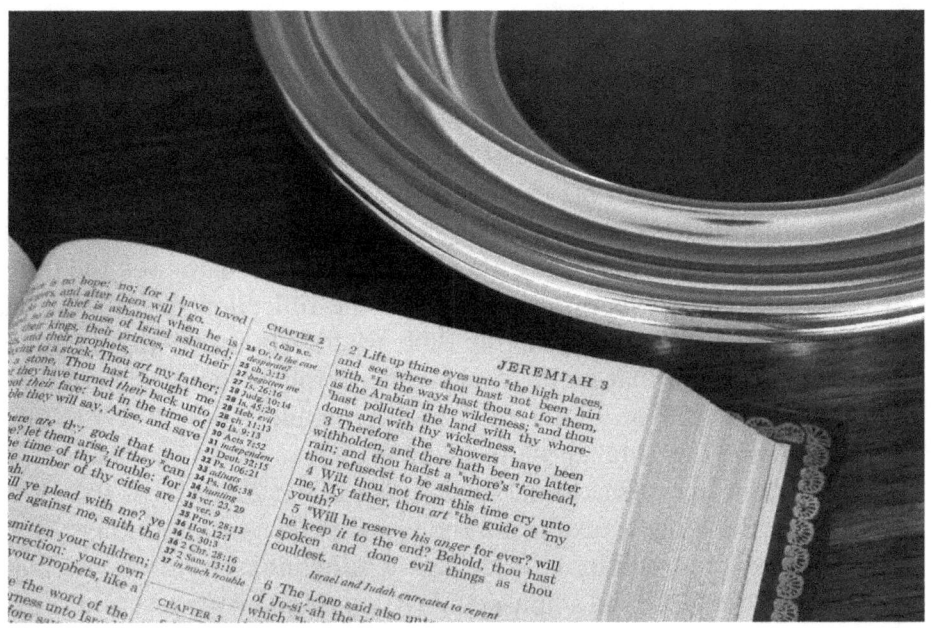

15.

The Blessings of Tithing

When God gave Abraham his great victory over the cohort of kings, Abraham was met on his return by an enigmatic priest, king, and prophet named Melchizedek. What is of particular interest about the encounter is that, after receiving his blessing, Abraham gave Melchizedek tithes (which is a tenth) of all the spoils that Abraham had taken from those he had overcome (Gen. 14:20). Many people have asked, "Why did Abraham do that? Where did he learn about the principles of tithing?"

One might not have all the answers, but one can be sure that Abraham must have been incredibly grateful for his signal victory. He only had 300 servants on his side to face the vast army of the four kings, but, by God's grace, he overcame them in a remarkable way. Thus, in returning a tithe, he acknowledged that he understood the source of his victory, and he also recognized that all he possessed was from God. What he had accomplished was not through his own strength, rather, it was from God. He paid the tithe to Melchizedek as an act of thankfulness and praise—it was an act of worship that was without coercion. Abraham took the tithe off the top of the spoils of war. Such was the reflection of his spirit of praise to God. We are not told in the Bible where Abraham's tithing came from, but it is noted that Jacob would come to follow the pattern of tithing (Gen. 28:20–22), and later the Israelites would follow it too (Num. 18:21–24; Lev. 27:30; Mal. 3:8–12). Likewise, it would also be observed in New Testament times (see Matt. 23:23; Luke 11:42; 2 Cor. 11:8, 9; 1 Cor. 9:16–18). In the longest text in the Bible that is focused on tithing (Mal. 3:8–12), there is a reminder to (a) bring the tithe into the storehouse that there may be food in God's house and (b) put God to the test and see if He will not open the windows of heaven and pour you out a blessing, so that you will not have room to receive it. Then, (c) all nations will call you blessed. Here are some of the lessons I have gathered from focusing on the blessings of tithing. Tithing—

- Acknowledges that God is the owner of the earth.
- Is the beginning of a journey with faith
- Tests our obedience to God
- Tests our attitude of gratitude versus any spirit of greed in us
- Tests how much we love God
- Tests our willingness to discipline ourselves to budget
- Tests our willingness to be honest with God. It is all about integrity of character
- Tests our willingness to deny self in response to God
- Tests our willingness to be in partnership with God
- Tests God—this is the one act in the Bible that offers human beings the privilege of testing God
- Teaches that we are called to give proportionately from what is in our possession. The poor is to return the tithe and the rich are also to return a tithe; no one is left out
- Allows God to rebuke the devourer for our sakes regarding the kinds of things that might destroy the fruits of our fields
- Preserves our vineyards—our properties—whatever they are

- Provides the way to God's abundance; God will "open the windows of heaven" and "pour out so many blessings that we will not have enough room to store them" (Mat. 3:10, NIRV)
- Increases our love for God
- Keeps our hearts tender and sympathetic
- Develops our character
- Tests our loyalty
- Brings us spiritual prosperity
- Enlivens us and brings happiness into our souls
- Brings us into a closer relationship with God
- Encourages our liberality, our generosity.

Yes, returning to God what is His brings untold blessings. In fact, returning to God opens the door to our attitude of giving versus focusing our hearts on only getting. I often make a point to those I have the privilege of pastoring when I say, "Don't pay tithe; return it." This is all we can do—return it to God who is the Giver of all gifts. He has placed us in the earth as stewards, and tithing is the least that we can do to show that we are faithful to our obligation of stewardship. Stewardship recognizes that God is the owner and we are the servants who are to keep and care for what God places in our hands, over which He has given us dominion and that we are to return to Him as He has requested. How faithful we intend to be is tested by our tithe. When God is honored with the tithe, God fulfills what He has promised—He opens the windows of heaven and pours out His blessings.

Take a Moment

Write down the blessing that the above reading has brought to your mind today, and whatever is your attitude about tithing.

_____
_____
_____
_____
_____
_____

Further, write down a special blessing that you would wish to ask the Lord to give you.

_____
_____
_____
_____
_____
_____

Then, write down how and with whom you would wish to share your blessing.

_____
_____
_____
_____
_____
_____

The Blessings of Aging

Then Abraham fell on his face and laughed, and said in his heart, "Shall a child be born to a man who is one hundred years old? And shall Sarah, who is ninety years old, bear a child?" (Gen. 17:17, NKJV)

Therefore Sarah laughed within herself, saying, "After I have grown old, shall I have pleasure, my lord being old also?" (Gen. 18:12, NKJV)

> Even in old age, with its aches and pains, we need to understand that, if God is directing our steps, we will be filled with multitudes of blessings.

16.

The Blessings of Aging

When we are young and full of vigor and the ocean of life's future stands before us, we often think that we are eternally blessed. But as the process of aging comes upon us and we come face to face with the trials of life and pain is reflected in the muscles of our being, we may tend to think, as did Solomon at the worst level of his frustration, that life is "vain." (See Solomon's reflections in Ecclesiastes). However, I want to use this present reflection to make the point that, while multiple blessings from God flow to the youth, they are also available in old age (see Ruth 4:15; Isa. 46:4; Job 12:12, 32:7).

One of the first mentioned blessings of old age is that which was given to Abraham. He was seventy-five years old when he received the promised blessing and was ninety-nine or a hundred years old—and Sarah was ninety—when God was working out His promise, blessing, "God said to Abraham, 'As for Sarai your wife, you shall not call her Sarai, but Sarah shall be her name. And I will bless her and also give you a son by her; then I will bless her, and she shall be a mother of nations; kings of peoples shall be from her.' Then Abraham fell on his face and laughed, and said in his heart, 'Shall a child be born to a man who is one hundred years old? And shall Sarah, who is ninety years old, bear a child?'" (Gen. 17:16, 17, NKJV). The story sounds crazy, doesn't it? Abraham certainly thought it crazy, and, later, Sarah also thought it crazy (see Genesis 18). You can see why Abraham fell on his face and laughed. He "mused" about a child being born to an old man and an old woman. *That's impossible!* he must have thought. I am sure that I would have laughed too or maybe even gone "berserker" than they did. But what Abraham and Sarah had to learn was what we all need to learn, namely, that God is not limited by our age or our logic. God is a boundary breaker and a way-maker. He can make dry paths through waters. He can go beyond the productions of scientific research. He works miracles. Miracles are not constructed in human logic. When God declares them, they happen,

> *But what Abraham and Sarah had to learn was what we all need to learn, namely, that God is not limited by our age or our logic.*

and faith anticipates them. What a joy to know that in bringing His blessings that God offers them to all who will believe! This is why Jesus said that, if you have faith as a grain of mustard seed, you will be able to remove mountains (Matt. 17:20).

For those who are thinking that they are getting too old to receive the blessings of God, let me make a list of the blessings of old age, some of which I gathered from an article in the *Huffington Post* and others from the Bible:

1. Perspective. One can look at life, not only from a forward perspective, but one can look back at life with a measured gaze.
2. Time. One can appreciate the present, understanding that the moment matters.
3. Freedom. One can stay out of the competition and enjoy one's life of liberation.
4. Newness. One can be spontaneous and creative without pressure of those about us.
5. Wisdom. One can share the wisdom that one has gained.
6. Living history. One can tell stories of life's journey and how it has been.
7. Relationships. One will find support in old relationships.
8. Meaning of life. One can focus on the true meaning of life—like Solomon said, "Let us hear the conclusion of the whole matter. Fear God" and give Him glory (Ecclesiastes 12:13, 14; Rev. 14:7).
9. Mature faith. One can spend more time with God without the constant rush of life.
10. Gray hair are a crown of glory or spender (Prov. 16:31; 20:29).
11. Opportunity to tell the next generation about the power and greatness of God in one's life (Ps. 71:18, 19).
12. Grandchildren are a crown of glory (Prov. 17:6).
13. One can appreciate one's length of days (Gen. 25:7, 8).
14. The extent of one's good health and strength (Deut. 34:7).

The point is that we are not to put our limits on God. Sometimes in our old age we feel limitations, but we need to remind ourselves of the comforting words of the prophet Isaiah: "And I'll keep on carrying you when you're old. I'll be there, bearing you when you're old and gray. I've done it and will keep on doing it, carrying you on my back, saving you" (Isa. 46:4, MSG). When we have aged, God does not forget us. He reminds the aged to exercise patience towards the young. Encourage them. Live with integrity and be exemplary. And He calls the young to honor the aged and take care of them.

Are you old or getting old? Take heart—you are still of value in the eyes of God. Old age is no barrier to God. It is a great time to receive and share God's blessings. That is one way to build a legacy.

Take a Moment

Write down the blessing that the above reading has brought to your mind today and for which you would wish to thank the Lord.
_____
_____
_____
_____
_____
_____

Further, write down a special blessing that you would wish to ask the Lord to give you.
_____
_____
_____
_____
_____
_____

Then, write down how and with whom you would wish to share your blessing.
_____
_____
_____
_____
_____
_____

The Blessings of Mercy

By Myself I have sworn, says the LORD, because you have done this thing, and have not withheld your son, your only son—blessings I will bless you, and multiplying I will multiply your descendants as the stars of the heaven and as the sand which is on the seashore; and your descendants shall possess the gate of their enemies. (Gen. 22:16, 17, NKJV)

> When we obey God's revealed Word, we are sure to receive a blessing. Satan hates it when we are blessed, and he will do all within his power to mess up our blessings. Nonetheless, while we submit to God, we are safe.

17.

The Blessings of Mercy

One of the more interesting stories in the Bible is that of Lot and his family—especially the part of the story connected with their rescue before the destruction of Sodom. At the heart of the story is how two angelic visitors entered Lot's house to advise him to leave the city. Lot welcomed the visitors into his house to share further hospitality. However, before Lot could share the customary favors, wicked men from the city surrounded the house and demanded that Lot allow them to rape the visitors. Lot was so confounded that he offered the evil men his two daughters. The evil men refused and kept beating down the door. Some Bible commentators have said it is hard for our modern sensibilities to understand why God would allow such a terrible incident to occur at Lot's house. Why would Lot offer his two daughters to the evil men? Why did God not stop the wicked men before they came to the door of the house? The questions are many, and there seem to be no clear answers. Yet, can we not see that God was most gracious in blinding the evil men and moving them from the door? "Then the men [the angel visitors] said to Lot, 'Have you anyone else here? Son-in-law, your sons, your daughters, and whomever you have in the city—take them out of this place! For we will destroy this place, because the outcry against them has grown great before the face of the LORD, and the LORD has sent us to destroy it.' So Lot went out and spoke to his sons-in-law, who had married his daughters, and said, 'Get up, get out of this place; for the LORD will destroy this city!' But to his sons-in-law he seemed to be joking" (Gen. 19:12–14, NKJV).

Yes, Lot accepted the urging of the angel visitors and went to speak to his sons-in-law who refused to leave the city. So, the visitors took Lot, his wife, and their two daughters and led them outside the city before the outbreak of fire that was to consume the city. The record states that, at a distance from the city, when Lot's wife looked back, she turned to "a pillar of salt" upon the "sight of God," who was descending down to rain destruction upon Sodom and Gomorrah (Gen. 19:26).

There are many lessons from the story to learn concerning divine judgment and mercy, but I direct my observations to lessons from Lot, namely—

1. How being hospitable can open the path of blessings to us and our families
2. How putting ourselves in untenable situations can have profound negative consequences for ourselves and our families
3. How failing to leave conditions of distractions can lead to the loss of our children
4. How failing to urgently act on our convictions may result in the loss of our loved ones.

Through God's mercy, we learn that He is ready to intervene in our situation.

1. God takes notice of our foolish choices and actions and intervenes to transform the curse into a blessing.
2. God is willing to save our family despite our imperfections.
3. God is always ready to use us as His channel of blessing to those around us.
4. God often rushes to rescue us from fires of destruction.

The name "Lot" means "veil" or "covering," and it is quite evident that his life in Sodom must have meant a covering for his family and neighbors. In fact, like Noah the evangelist who preached to the Antediluvians in the hope of saving them from the flood (see Gen. 6 and 7), Lot preached to the people of Sodom and Gomorrah to save them from the fires of destruction. But the people rejected the message of Lot, and, when their sins reached to "the highest heaven," God turned His anger against the cities to consume them. In reflecting on the fires, the apostle Peter says that God "delivered righteous Lot, who was oppressed by the filthy conduct of the wicked (for that righteous man, dwelling among them, tormented his righteous soul from day to day by seeing and hearing their lawless deeds)—then the Lord knows how to deliver the godly out of temptations and to reserve the unjust under punishment for the day of judgment" (2 Peter 2:7–9, NKJV).

Alongside the expression of God's judgment in the consuming fires of Sodom there are evidences of God's mercy. The lyrics of a popular Christian song, written by James H. Filmore, say:

I will sing of the mercies of the Lord forever,
I will sing, I will sing;
I will sing of the mercies of the Lord forever,
I will sing of the mercies of the Lord.
With my mouth will I make known
Thy faithfulness, Thy faithfulness,
With my mouth will I make known
Thy faithfulness to all generations.
I will sing of the mercies of the Lord forever,
I will sing of the mercies of the Lord.

Just imagine the blessings of mercy that we would often receive if we treated those who come into our way like angels. Yes, it is true, "angels that excel in strength" are always coming and going with blessings from heaven to give to us. As it is said, they take our prayers to heaven and then bring us back God's blessings.

Take a Moment

Write down the blessing that the above reading has brought to your mind today and for which you would wish to thank the Lord.

_____
_____
_____
_____
_____
_____

Further, write down a special blessing that you would wish to ask the Lord to give you.

_____
_____
_____
_____
_____
_____

Then, write down how and with whom you would wish to share your blessing.

_____
_____
_____
_____
_____
_____

The Blessings of Godly Relationships

Therefore a man shall leave his father and mother and be joined to his wife, and they shall become one flesh. (Gen. 2:24, NKJV)

> God will not bless a relationship in which He is not involved. No matter how strong the relationship might seem, it will fall apart without God.

18.

The Blessings of Godly Relationships

Some time ago, I found myself in the company of two men who had married nine women. After speaking to them, I began to think of my parents' blessing of having been married for 71 years. I also thought of my own marriage and that of my sister—50 years of marriage for each of us. Mom died seven years before Dad, but Dad insisted that he could never marry again. He did not mean this because he was 98 years of age, for he lived to nearly 105. He meant it because, speaking often of my mother as the love of his life, it was as if she were the only woman that ever existed in the world. In listening to Dad, one would think that their relationship was "a relationship made in heaven." He also often made it seem that all their children's successes were attributable to Mom. We know better. But what is evident is that our parents had the highest regard for each other. They were great collaborators. Even though Dad spent a lot of time working away from home, he and Mom were always a team. Is it that they were more blessed than the men and women that we have met whose relationships seem broken and miserable? Is it that only a few of us have the staying power to be able to give praise about how blessed we are from staying together?

For all I have read from social history, marriages have always been breaking up, perhaps not as easily as they are breaking up these days, but they have been breaking up nonetheless. Moreover, the people of God have been continually warned not to adopt the world's way of making and breaking relationships. Solomon wrote, "Rejoice in the wife of your youth" (Prov. 5:18, NIV). Malachi says, "and this is the second thing you do: You cover the altar of the LORD with tears, with weeping and crying; so He does not regard the offering anymore, nor receive it with goodwill from your hands. Yet you say, 'For what reason?' Because the LORD has been witnessing between you and the wife of your youth, with whom you have dealt treacherously; yet she is your companion and your wife by covenant" (Mal. 2:13, 14, NKJV). In dealing with the scribes regarding the question of divorce, Jesus quoted the Genesis account given to the first married couple, "Have you not read that He who made them at the beginning 'made them male and female,' For this reason a man shall leave his father and mother and be joined to his wife, and the two shall become one flesh'? So then, they are no longer two but one flesh. Therefore, what God has joined together, let not man separate" (Matt. 19:4–7, NKJV). Jesus' point is that the covenant of marriage is expected to last forever—"until death do us part."

If marriage were treated today as a blessing, as it was offered to humanity in the beginning (see Gen. 2:18–25), it would be more seriously cherished. The choice of a mate made in one's youth would be treated with higher regard, and relationships would be more seriously nurtured. It might seem harsh, but here is what I offered one of the two men I mentioned as having married nine times:

- If it ever comes into your mind to marry again, think seriously whether it is truly what you need to do.

- If you ever think of getting married again, pray for God to help you to be transformed. Don't try to change the one you marry.
- Stop searching for the right person. You might be looking too far. Life is not always about the other person. It might be about you.
- Open yourself to divine guidance. God will give you wisdom to know the difference.
- Seek the will of God. Listen to what He instructs, for He is extremely interested in godly relationships.
- Never forget that God wants to bless your marriage, but if He is not at the center, He cannot bless it.

The point I am making is that our relationships are intended to be a blessing not only to us but to anyone we have chosen to marry and to the generations that are produced by the marriage. Blessings create stability and make us channels of blessings to those who follow us. Our marriages might not be made in heaven, for, while they are made on earth, they can make us feel like we are getting a touch of heaven.

Take a Moment

Write down the blessing that the above reading has brought to your mind today and for which you would wish to thank the Lord.

_____
_____
_____
_____
_____

Further, write down a special blessing that you would wish to ask the Lord to give you.

_____
_____
_____
_____
_____

Then, write down how and with whom you would wish to share your blessing.

_____
_____
_____
_____
_____

She Will Be a Blessing to You

And they blessed Rebekah and said to her,
our sister, *may* you *become*
The mother of thousands of ten thousands;
And may your descendants possess
The gates of those who hate them.
(Gen. 24:60, NKJV)

> When we bless others, we create a cycle of blessings. We are blessed to bless, we set in motion a legacy of blessings to the generations beyond ours.

19.

She Will Be a Blessing to You

If you had been following my life's story over the years, you would likely have heard or seen the many references I have made to the question that one of my college faculty mentors asked me. My mentor was interested in knowing my feelings about the young lady to whom she saw I was showing some interest. After hearing my response, she said to me, "I think she will be good for you."

Good for me? I mused.

Anyone who knows me understands that such a suggestion would leave me in deep contemplation. I did marry that very young lady about whom my mentor spoke. But, in doing so, I went back to my mentor about six times to clarify what she meant by "she will be good for you," and my mentor simply responded with smiles. Maybe she did not know what to make of her own intuition other than what she later said, "I told you so. See, you and your wife are together for 50 years now." What I know is that, although my mentor's intuition was most powerful, I also credit our longevity to the eternal blessings of God. Such blessings have held our lives together. After my mentor had given her affirmation, my mother, father, aunt, and the sister that follows me in the family lineage were also quite impressed with the young lady and encouraged me in my choice.

How many people, these days, are blessed as I have been? I cannot say, but I am convinced that many could use some of the same kinds of blessings and affirmations. My story leads me to think of the story of how Rebecca became the wife of Isaac. The full story is told in Genesis 24 and is quite lengthy, but here are some highlights:

- Abraham was getting quite old.
- Before his death, he wanted to see Isaac married to a wife who loved the Lord.
- He called his servant Eliezer, who was in charge of his house, to get a wife for Isaac.

- He told Eliezer to go back to his homeland and family in Haran to find the right wife.
- Eliezer was willing to go but doubted that he would find the right woman who would be willing to follow him back to Canaan.
- As Eliezer shared his fear, Abraham pressed back upon him and he followed his instructions.
- Abraham required an oath of Eliezer, asking him to put his hand under Abraham's rib.
- Then Eliezer went on the journey.
- Along the way, Eliezer paused to pray that God would guide him.
- In the prayer, he asked God to show him through a test who was the right person.
- The test worked, and he was able to identify the young lady the Lord wanted him to meet. Her name was Rebekah.
- He asked her to take him to meet her family. She was the daughter of Nahor, Abraham's brother.
- When the young lady accepted his invitation, Eliezer blessed the Lord for His guidance and he blessed Abraham for his insights. He had been successful in finding the right one.
- On reaching the Rebekah's home, Eliezer recited to the family how God had blessed Abraham. Then he told of the mission on which he had been sent, the oath he had taken, and how he had come to the well where the women drew water for their animals. He recounted his prayer to God to find the right wife for his master's son, Isaac. Then he described how he met Rebekah at the well and that she had accepted his proposal on behalf of his master, and he repeated the blessing that he gave to God in appreciation for the accepted proposal.
- He concluded with a request for Nahor and his family to endorse what God had done. The family endorsed the idea and the offer of gifts to Rebekah to travel with him to where Isaac and Abraham lived. We hear their delight. "And they blessed Rebekah and said to her: 'Our sister, may you become the mother of thousands of ten thousands, and may your descendants possess the gates of those who hate them' " (Gen. 24:60).

Although we might find the cultural mode of the formation of a relationship quite antiquated, we can still learn multiple lessons from it. Such lessons will not be included here because of space limitations. However, one might ask the following questions: (1) What part does divine choice play in our mate selections today? (2) Do we want to know what the will of God is? (3) Will we listen to the impressions God gives in this regard? It is essential to state that God sends His affirmations through parents and many otherwise people around us. The wisdom and experience of age have been a blessing to many generations, and can still be useful today. Let us carefully check some of the ways that God acts in relationship building.

1. "He who finds a wife finds a good thing, and obtains favor from the LORD" (Prov. 18:22, NKJV).
2. "Who can find a virtuous wife? For her worth is far above rubies" (Prov. 31:10, NKJV).
3. "For the husband is head of the wife, as also Christ is head of the church; and He is the Savior of the body" (Eph. 5:23, NKJV).
4. "It is good for a man not to touch a woman. Nevertheless, because of sexual immorality, let each man have his own wife, and let each woman have her own husband. Let the husband render to his wife the affection due her, and likewise also the wife to her husband" (1 Cor. 7:1–3, NKJV).
5. "Let your fountain be blessed, and rejoice with the wife of your youth. As a loving deer and a graceful doe, let her breasts satisfy you at all times; And always be enraptured with her love" (Prov. 5:18, 19, NKJV).
6. "Live joyfully with the wife whom you love all the days of your vain life which He has given you under the sun, all your days of vanity; for that is your portion in life, and in the labor which you perform under the sun" (Eccles. 9:9, NKJV).
7. "An excellent wife is the crown of her husband, but she who causes shame is like rottenness in his bones" (Prov. 12:4, NKJV).
8. "And be kind to one another, tenderhearted, forgiving one another, even as God in Christ forgave you" (Eph. 4:32, NKJV).

My concluding point of interest is to ask whether, in the building of a relationship, you think it is worthwhile to take or seek advice. In the book of Proverbs, we are told that a wise person will seek out counsel (1:5) to gain understanding (19:20) because such will make him or her happy (18:2). I give my thanks to the ones who were so helpful to me more than 50 years ago.

Take a Moment

Write down the blessing that the above reading has brought to your mind today and for which you would wish to thank the Lord.

_____
_____
_____
_____
_____

Further, write down a special blessing that you would wish to ask the Lord to give you.

_____
_____
_____
_____
_____

Then, write down how and with whom you would wish to share your blessing.

_____
_____
_____
_____
_____

Passing On the Blessings

"And it came to pass, after the death of Abraham, that God blessed his son Isaac. And Isaac dwelt at Beer Lahoi Roi." (Gen. 25:11, NKJV)

"And Abraham gave all that he had to Isaac. But Abraham gave gifts to the sons of the concubines which Abraham had; and while he was still living he sent them eastward, away from Isaac his son, to the country of the east." (Gen. 25:5, 6, NKJV)

> It is a supreme task of parenting to bless our children. When we bless our children, the blessings will flow to future generations. If parents curse their children, the curse will also flow to future generations.

20.

Passing On the Blessings

After watching the successful "March for Our Lives," of nearly one million students and youths in Washington, DC, in other American cities, and in many other cities around the world, I was led to ask once again about the legacies that many parents are passing on to their children. Are we leaving our children to fend for and defend themselves under the threat of guns? or, are we giving them the blessed protection of divine grace that they need so that they can survive into the next generation?

You might be surprised by the biblical story that I see connected to the "March for Our Lives," but it struck me when I read, "And it came to pass, after the death of Abraham, that God blessed his son Isaac. And Isaac dwelt at Beer Lahai Roi" (Gen. 25:11, NKJV). An earlier part of the story says, "And Abraham gave all that he had to Isaac. But Abraham gave gifts to the sons of the concubines which Abraham had; and while he was still living he sent them eastward, away from Isaac his son, to the country of the east" (Gen. 25:5, 6, NKJV).

Before focusing on the point that I wish to make about how God blessed Isaac, I take note of the fact that Abraham gave "all he had to Isaac" as well as "gifts to his other sons." Although it baffles me a bit, I think it exemplary. What he did is not like one father, I met, who argued that he had already given his children all that he wished to give them. When I asked him what he meant, he said that he had given them life and that was all he owed them. Their mother should now take care of the rest. I was so disgusted that I walked away, for he reminded me of too many fathers who have abandoned their sons and daughters, leaving them to fend for themselves. Young people are frightened, fearful, and frustrated. They do not think that they have a great future in a society that lets fathers off the hook without expecting them to be responsible for their children.

But let us return to the story of the blessing that Abraham gave Isaac and that Isaac was to pass on. Even though Abraham was dying, he secured the blessing for the son that God told him would carry on the covenant blessing. When it was Isaac's turn to pass on the blessing, Isaac vacillated between his two sons. He wanted to pass on the blessing to Esau, the son he favored, rather than to Jacob, who was predicted to be the covenant son. Rebekah, on the other hand, in her impatience to push Isaac to follow the prediction, initiated a scheme that could get Jacob, her favored son, the blessing. After the scheme was carried out, the resentment and animus in the home became so severe that, to avoid the murder that might have taken place, Jacob was sent away to live with his uncle Laban in Padan Aran. In fact, having left home, Jacob never saw his mother again. She died before his return, and he did not attend her burial.

There is no question that, in the history of the generations that would come from Isaac, many other difficulties would be confronted, and only through the grace of God would the blessings continue through the Messiah. That means that, when God adds His blessing to any person or situation, there may be times when the blessing is turned into a curse. Yet, by His grace, God can bring restoration, taking away the curse and turning it into a blessing. Of course, we can avoid turning our blessing into a curse if we will follow the way that God is seeking to guide us rather than using our own strategic direction to secure the blessing.

1. We need to avoid the philosophy that holds that we will receive the blessing by just trying much harder.
2. Parents also need to note the damage they might be doing when they try to share blessings based on favoritism. With lack of care, parents can leave a whole generation of their progeny in conflict.
3. If one person takes advantage of another to secure God's blessing, the first person might feel comfortable for a while, but ultimately he or she will lose the blessing.
4. Just because a person receives God's blessing does not mean that the person is righteous. In the gospel of Matthew, we are told that God "causes his sun to rise on the evil and the good, and sends rain on the righteous and the unrighteous" (Matt. 5:45, TLV).

In effect, God wants everyone to receive His blessings, but it is up to us how we share the blessings. In serving as God's channels of blessings, we need to be wise, and we need to listen to the directions that He gives us.

Take a Moment

Write down the blessing that the above reading has brought to your mind today and for which you would wish to thank the Lord.

_____
_____
_____
_____
_____

Further, write down a special blessing that you would wish to ask the Lord to give you.

_____
_____
_____
_____
_____

Then, write down how and with whom you would wish to share your blessing.

_____
_____
_____
_____
_____

Don't Throw Away Your Blessings

Now Jacob cooked a stew; and Esau came in from the field, and he was weary. And Esau said to Jacob, "Please feed me with that same red stew, for I am weary." Therefore his name was called Edom. But Jacob said, "Sell me your birthright as of this day." And Esau said, "Look, I am about to die; so, what is this birthright to me?" Then Jacob said, "Swear to me as of this day." So he swore to him, and sold his birthright to Jacob. And Jacob gave Esau bread and stew of lentils; then he ate and drank, arose, and went his way. Thus Esau despised his birthright. (Gen. 25:29–33, NKJV)

> Just think for a minute how many people in the world are missing opportunities in their lives to secure their blessings. Many are so focused on their present that they miss their future.

21.

Don't Throw Away Your Blessings

Have you ever taken a lot of time to buy a gift you considered a thing of great value for a child, and then noticed that the child, not knowing the value of the gift, destroyed the gift within a short time? You must have felt really sad, if not angry.

Consider the trajectory of your emotions and then think of the way that Isaac must have felt when he came to learn that Esau squandered his birthright to Jacob for a "bowl of pottage." The story is profoundly fascinating. A part of the story reads as follows:

> Now Jacob cooked a stew; and Esau came in from the field, and he was weary. And Esau said to Jacob, "Please feed me with that same red stew, for I am weary." Therefore, his name was called Edom. But Jacob said, "Sell me your birthright as of this day." And Esau said, "Look, I am about to die; so, what is this birthright to me?" Then Jacob said, "Swear to me as of this day." So, he swore to him, and sold his birthright to Jacob. And Jacob gave Esau bread and stew of lentils; then he ate and drank, arose, and went his way. Thus Esau despised his birthright. (Gen. 25:29–34, NKJV)

You might be angry at Jacob for taking advantage of Esau at the moment of his greatest vulnerability. Or you might be sad for Esau for being as foolish as he was. He must have been starving. Maybe all the blood was drained away from his head. He could not think. Or could he? In his vanity or greed, he sought to satisfy his most basic instinct rather than thinking of his destiny. In order to satisfy his immediate need, the thought of preserving his birthright or inheritance was not important. What was a birthright to a hungry stomach? This is a question that Jesus had to face at the end of his forty-day fast (see Matt. 4:3). Jesus was famished and the devil thought that He could use His condition to have Him turn stones into bread, but Jesus would not yield.

We can frame several questions to Esau and forget Jacob for a moment because to focus on Jacob all the time is to pass blame. Esau needed to take responsibility. He needed to learn to appreciate his birthright. It would give him the property of his father and the place of priority in the family. However, he had no vision and wagered his future on present gratification.

Many have thrown away the greatest blessings of their lives in the same way that Esau did. This is why the author of Hebrews makes the appeal:

> Looking carefully lest anyone fall short of the grace of God; lest any root of bitterness springing up cause trouble, and by this many become defiled; lest there be any fornicator or profane person like Esau, who for one morsel of food sold his birthright. For you know that afterward, when he wanted to inherit the blessing, he was rejected, for he found no place for repentance, though he sought it diligently with tears. (Heb. 12:15–17, NKJV)

The above appeal prompts such questions as:

- How often have our emotions driven us to do self-destructive things?
- What are the blessings of God that we have thrown away?
- How often do we think in the short-term instead of the long-term?
- How much do we live in time instead of eternity?
- What have we exchanged for our soul's salvation?
- Is money of more value to us than morality?
- Does worldly success mean more than our spiritual well-being?

One commentator has said that Esau had lightly valued the blessing while it seemed within his reach, but, after it was gone from him, his grief and rage were terrible. He said, "Bless me, even me also, O my father!" "Hast thou not reserved a blessing for me?" (Gen. 27:38, 6, KJV). But the birthright which he had so carelessly bartered, he could not regain. "For one morsel of meat" (Heb. 12:16, KJV), for a momentary gratification of appetite that had never been restrained, Esau sold his inheritance. When Esau "saw his folly, it was too late to recover the blessing. 'He found no place of repentance, though he sought it carefully with tears.' Hebrews 12:17. Esau was not shut out from seeking God's favor by repentance, but he was not able to find any means of recovering the birthright. His grief did not spring from conviction of sin; he did not desire to be reconciled to God" (Ellen G. White, *From Eternity Past*, p. 117).

There are lots of inheritance advisers around. They are needed because many people do not know how to manage their inheritance. They are throwing their inheritance away. About one third of inheritors throw away their inheritance. Since this is the case with temporal inheritance, just imagine what is happening with their eternal inheritance. Are we throwing away our inheritance?

Take a Moment

Write down any blessing that the Lord has given to you, and think of any you seem to be throwing away.

_____
_____
_____
_____
_____
_____

Further, write down a special blessing that you would wish to ask the Lord to pour upon you.

_____
_____
_____
_____
_____
_____

Then, write down how and with whom you would wish to share your blessing.

_____
_____
_____
_____
_____
_____

The Blessings of Peacemaking

So Isaac moved away from there and encamped in the Valley of Gerar, where he settled. Isaac reopened the wells that had been dug in the time of his father Abraham, which the Philistines had stopped up after Abraham died, and he gave them the same names his father had given them. Isaac's servants dug in the valley and discovered a well of fresh water there. But the herders of Gerar quarreled with those of Isaac and said, "The water is ours!" So he named the well Esek, because they disputed with him. Then they dug another well, but they quarreled over that one also; so he named it Sitnah. He moved on from there and dug another well, and no one quarreled over it. He named it Rehoboth, saying, "Now the LORD has given us room and we will flourish in the land." From there he went up to Beersheba. That night the LORD appeared to him and said, "I am the God of your father Abraham. Do not be afraid, for I am with you; I will bless you and will increase the number of your descendants for the sake of my servant Abraham." Isaac built an altar there and called on the name of the LORD. There he pitched his tent, and there his servants dug a well.

Meanwhile, Abimelech had come to him from Gerar, with Ahuzzath his personal adviser and Phichol the commander of his forces. Isaac asked them, "Why have you come to me, since you were hostile to me and sent me away?"

They answered, "We saw clearly that the Lord was with you; so we said, 'There ought to be a sworn agreement between us'—between us and you. Let us make a treaty with you that you will do us no harm, just as we did not harm you but always treated you well and sent you away peacefully. And now you are blessed by the Lord." Isaac then made a feast for them, and they ate and drank. Early the next morning the men swore an oath to each other. Then Isaac sent them on their way, and they went away peacefully. That day Isaac's servants came and told him about the well they had dug. They said, "We've found water!" He called it Shibah, and to this day the name of the town has been Beersheba. (Gen. 26:17–33, NIV)

> Don't take your blessings for granted. When you take a shower or even drink a glass of cold water to quench your thirst, say, "Blessed be the Lord."

22.

The Blessings of Peacemaking

After looking at our contemporary conditions across the world, particularly the pride of nations, the internal strife between racial and ethnic communities, the prejudice, the competition, the meanness, the hatred, and the passion for warfare, I have been wondering out loud, "How many of us would be like Isaac?" There is a reference to a particular part of his life, recorded in Genesis 26:17–33, that strikes me deeply. It tells how he went to live in the valley of Gerar where he re- dug the wells that had been dug in the days of his father Abraham. The Philistines had stopped up the wells after Abraham's death, but Isaac re-dug the wells and called them by the same names his father had given them. His servants also dug other wells in the valley and found one well of running water. But, as the issue is today, there was struggle over water. The story tells us that "the herdsmen of Gerar quarreled with Isaac's herdsmen, saying, 'The water is ours.' So he called the name of the well Esek... Then they dug another well, and they quarreled over that one also. So he called its name Sitnah. And he moved from there and dug another well, and they did not quarrel over it. So he called its name Rehoboth, because he said, 'For now the LORD has made room for us, and we shall be fruitful in the land' " (Gen. 26:20-22, NKJV).

The rest of the story is that, as Isaac went up from Beersheba, the Lord appeared to him the same night and said, "I am the God of your father Abraham; do not fear, for I am with you. I will bless you and multiply your descendants for My servant Abraham's sake" (Gen. 26:24, NKJV). Isaac therefore built an altar and called on the name of the Lord, and he pitched his tent, and his servants dug another well. King Abimelech, who had driven Isaac away, saw how God had blessed him. The king left Gerar with Ahuzzath, one of his friends, and Phichol, the commander of his army to find Isaac. He went to make peace. King Abimelech did what the common expression states: "If you can't beat them, join them." He sought peace with Isaac. One Proverb states, "When a man's ways please the LORD, he makes even his enemies be at peace with him" (Prov. 16:7, ESV). Isaac, knowing the treatment he had received from the king, wondered why he and his men had come to see him. Thus, Isaac asked, "Why have you come to me, since you hate me and have sent me away from you?" "But they said, 'We have certainly seen that the LORD is with you.' " They also said, " 'Let there now be an oath between us, between you and us; and let us make a covenant with you, that you will do us no harm, since we have not touched you, and since we have done nothing to you but good and have sent you away in peace. You are now the blessed of the LORD' " (Gen. 26:27–29, NKJV). Reflect, for a moment, on the noble attitude of Isaac. He made a feast for king Abimelech and his men. They ate and drank together, then the king and his men left early the next morning. Before leaving, Isaac and King Abimelech swore oaths to each other; and the king left in peace. On the same day that king Abimelech and his men left, Isaac's servants told him about the well they had dug. They had found water, and Isaac named the well "Sheba," which was later called "Beersheba," which means "well of the oath" or "well of the seven."

When people are mean to me, and frustration overtakes me, I have had to pray, "Lord, I want to be like Isaac—making peace. The world around me needs more men like him. With all of the saber-rattling, all of the missiles waiting to be launched without a thought of who might be hurt, Lord, make me like Isaac." Without an awakening of our consciences to tell us what we are doing to ourselves, we are certainly going to self-destruct. Mind you, no one needs to be a doormat, for people to walk upon, but we need to be aware that much of our outrage and reaction to provocation cannot help with relationship building. *Lord, teach us conflict management so that we can fill the earth with peace.*

Yes, while we need to speak to those around us concerning their rage and reaction, we also need to speak to ourselves in little ways by asking what are we doing to create peace? Remember what Jesus said, "Blessed are the peacemakers, for they will be called children of God" (Matt. 5:9, NIV). Jesus also said, "When you enter a house, first say, 'Peace to this house.' If someone who promotes peace is there, your peace will rest on them; if not, it will return to you" (Luke 10:5, 6, NIV). The fact is: if they do not want peace, that is their problem, not yours. Not everyone in the world wants peace, but our job is to promote peacemaking. Build bridges. Dig wells. Heal hearts. You might never receive a peace prize from the world's organizations that promote peace, but God will take note and register your name in His book that, like Isaac, you did all you could to make peace. If you cannot do anything more to bring peace, just pray for peace.

> *Mind you, no one needs to be a doormat, for people to walk upon, but we need to be aware that much of our outrage and reaction to provocation cannot help with relationship building.*

Take a Moment

Write down the blessing that the above reading has brought to your mind today and for which you would wish to thank the Lord.

_____
_____
_____
_____
_____

Further, write down a special blessing that you would wish to ask the Lord to give you.

_____
_____
_____
_____
_____

Then, write down how and with whom you would wish to share your blessing.

_____
_____
_____
_____
_____

God Bless You My Son

So he went to him and kissed him.

When Isaac caught the smell of his clothes, he blessed him and said,

"Ah, the smell of my son is like the smell of a field that the Lord has blessed.

May God give you heaven's dew and of earth's richness—

an abundance of grain and new wine.

May nations serve you and peoples bow down to you.

Be lord over your brothers, and may the sons of your mother bow down to you.

May those who curse you be cursed and those who bless you be blessed."

(Genesis 27:27–29, NIV)

> God has given fathers powerful opportunities to speak blessings into the lives of their children. The greatest task of fathers is to shape the lives of their children. This tops the blessings. At the foundation of the blessings is the call to speak over the children the word of God.

23.

God Bless You My Son

May I ask you, as a parent, when last have you raised your hand and pronounced a blessing on your son or daughter or on someone you seek to mentor? Many children today are waiting for such a blessing. They need a hand to be raised over them, to protect them, to encourage them, to make them feel that someone is present for them. It is unfortunate how many are living under a curse. Because of the selfishness of so many parents, multiple curses are being passed from generation to generation. Thank God that, through His mercies, He has been using alternative means for many children to receive His blessings.

The story of how Jacob received the covenant blessing and how Esau received a general blessing is always disconcerting to many individuals. As told in Genesis 27, Isaac sent Esau on a hunt for deer meat (called in some Bible translations, venison). He intended to pass on the covenant blessing to Esau (vss. 1–5). Of course, Rebekah, Isaac's wife, had a different idea. She plotted with Jacob how to obtain the blessing (vss. 6–17). Following Rebekah's instruction, Jacob pretended to be Esau, and obtained the blessing (vss. 18–29). When Esau returned from the hunt and went to Isaac to receive his blessing, Isaac revealed that the blessing was already passed to Jacob and could not be taken back. Isaac then offered Esau a general blessing (vss. 30–40). But Esau felt cheated and threatened Jacob's life, so that Rebekah sent Jacob away to her brother in Padan Aram (vss. 41–46).

The story is full of intrigue. Someone says, "It was one of those crooked measures often adopted to further the divine promises, as if the end would justify or excuse wrong means." But the problem was that Father Isaac was so attached to Esau that he did all he could to resist the divine direction. He was going to force the blessing upon Esau, regardless of his knowledge of what God had directed. On the other hand, Mother Rebekah decided to take things into her own hands to guide the blessing to Jacob. Both parents acted wrongly. Even though the divine purpose was fulfilled when Jacob received the covenant blessing, yet the family was left in disarray as Esau hated Jacob for the deception. Only a divine intervention would later transform their situation so that they were able to forgive each other and live (though apart from one another) as brothers.

Without trying to trivialize the intrigue or wrong actions of all those involved in the saga of Isaac, Rebekah, Jacob, and Esau, I return to the point raised in my introduction, "When last have you raised your hand and pronounced a blessing on your son or daughter or mentee?" How do you think Jacob felt when he went up to his father and heard the poetry of blessing being recited over his head? As we read in the story:

> So he [Jacob] went to him and kissed him [Isaac]. When Isaac caught the smell of his clothes, he blessed him and said, "Ah, the smell of my son is like the smell of a field that the LORD has blessed. May God give you heaven's dew and earth's richness—an abundance of grain and new wine. May nations serve you and peoples bow down to you. Be lord over your brothers, and may the sons of your mother bow down to you. May those who curse you be cursed and those who bless you be blessed." (Gen. 27:27–29, NIV)

What a blessing! You do not have to say what Isaac said, but, in multiple ways, you can pass on a legacy of blessings to your children and others. Learn who they are or what the destiny that God has for their lives. Here are 27 blessings that I have noted over the years that we can offer to others.

1. Temporal blessings of protection and provision.
2. Spiritual blessings—giving the priesthood blessings that come from heaven.
3. Teaching them reverence and respect—what it means to worship God.
4. Teaching how to be mature and what it means to respect others.
5. Teaching them courage—what is called bold virtue. Many of our children's cares, fears, and anxieties are what we teach them. They will live more courageously if they see it in practice.
6. Teaching them compassion. Courage and compassion are not in contradiction—men also need to show that they "have a heart," that they can be emphatic.
7. Giving fatherly advice—say, "My son, or my daughter, I don't think that is—or will be—good for you."
8. Showing them the meaning of life's purpose—what life is all about—that life has meaning when directed to the divine destiny.
9. Teaching them the blessings of relationship—how to relate to other men and women.

10. Expressing pleasure at their successes. How does it feel when a father can say to a child, "I am proud of you, my son, or my daughter"?
11. Praying for their wisdom—that they may be able to judge things correctly.
12. Teaching them how to pray—that their saying, "Abba Father, who art in heaven," might mean something special. Many children have difficulty relating to the heavenly Father because their earthly father has given them such a bad picture.
13. Loving them—the importance of a father's love on personality development in children is being trivialized today because humanity has rejected the divine model of fatherhood and motherhood. But hundreds of studies have shown that a father's love is as important as a mother's love and, at times, might be *more* critical than a mothers' love in personality development. One study argued that the importance of a father's love helps motivate many men to become more involved in nurturing and childcare. Further, widespread recognition of the influence of fathers on their children's personality development reduces the incidence of "mother blaming," which is common in schools and clinical settings. The same study argues: "The great emphasis on mothers and mothering in America has led to an inappropriate tendency to blame mothers for children's behavior problems and maladjustment when, in fact, fathers are often more implicated than mothers in the development of problems such as these" (Ronald Rohner, "Transnational Relations Between Perceived Parental Acceptance and Personality Dispositions of Children and Adults: A Meta-Analytic Review," *Personality and Social Psychology Review*, Sept. 1, 2011).
14. The blessing of naming them—here is one of the highest privileges that fathers have to name their children. In the western world (whenever the father is known), the child always gets the name of that father. It is a tragedy that so many mothers have to use paternity tests to determine the identity of the father because men have failed to be responsible.
15. Speaking to their strengths—to do so we need to take time to know the person and build him or her up.
16. Showing them consistency. One of the best ways to teach consistency is to model it.
17. Teaching them accountability. Do you take responsibility for your actions, or are you one of those men that like to make excuses and blame others?

18. Teaching them integrity and honesty—answering the question: Can you face yourself?
19. Teaching them anger management.
20. Teaching them self-sacrifice—there are plenty of self-aggrandizing men in the world.
21. Teaching them self-discipline—that is, the ability to control oneself and work hard or behave in a particular way without needing anyone else to say what to do.
22. Teaching them patience. Many people in the world fly into a rage when things do not go their way. How does a patient adult react to life? Your child needs to know.
23. Teaching them how to deal with suffering. Some people have never learned how to face trials; they become frustrated too quickly because they have never seen how others deal with their frustrations.
24. Teaching them self-denial, for self-denial begins with a proper sense of the holiness of God. It puts God first and foremost in everything. It means obedience and loyalty to God.
25. Teaching them how to use their freedoms, their power of choice.
26. Repeating to them the stories of your life. Tell of how God has been merciful despite where you have been.
27. Making sure they understand what it means to have presence—the warmth of sharing their authentic lives with others.

God has blessings planned for every child, every person. As parents, guardians, and mentors, it is our task to learn what such blessings are and to affirm them. Do not allow an opportunity to slip by without passing on a blessing, for we are the channels of life that God has chosen to pass on blessings. Do not wait until you are as old as Isaac before passing on the blessing. It might be too late, or you might be somewhat confused about which child you want to direct your blessing to. Isaac was about 135 years of age, and his sons about 75. He was blind and seemed confused. Although it was late, he still tried, and, while he did not fulfill his desire to bless the eldest, he did fulfill God's desire. In this, you might say, "It is never too late for a rain shower," because you never know what your opportunities will be. But do not take comfort in holding back God's blessings. Bless your children early and often. Say "God bless you, my son, my daughter." "God bless you, my friend." "God bless you. God bless you."

Take a Moment

Write down the blessing that the above reading has brought to your mind today and for which you would wish to thank the Lord.

_____
_____
_____
_____
_____

Further, write down a special blessing that you would wish to ask the Lord to give you.

_____
_____
_____
_____
_____

Then, write down how and with whom you would wish to share your blessing.

_____
_____
_____
_____
_____

Resented for Being Blessed

"So Esau hated Jacob because of the blessing with which his father blessed him, and Esau said in his heart, 'The days of mourning for my father are at hand; then I will kill my brother Jacob.' " (Gen. 27:41, NKJV)

> People might hate you for your blessings, but they cannot take them away from you when you are under the mighty hand of God.

24.

Resented for Being Blessed

Can you believe how much resentment there is in the world, especially against those who are blessed? Whenever I read the part of the Bible text that says, "So Esau hated Jacob because of the blessing with which his father blessed him" (Gen. 27:41, NKJV), it makes me think of the rising current of hatred in our present world. I think especially of what is happening to individuals who are standing up for decency, integrity, morality, justice, and faith in Jesus Christ.

I recognize that hatred is nothing new. It has been at the heart of Satan's playbook since the beginning of time. For example, Cain directed it against Abel because God blessed Abel for the sacrifice he offered, while Cain, who decided to offer up the kind of sacrifice that was not required, did not get the blessing (Gen. 4). It was also directed against Israel while they lived in Egypt and Persia. In Egypt, they were profoundly blessed, but, after the death of Joseph, the old Israelite governor, a new Pharaoh came to the throne. The new pharaoh became so jealous that he enslaved Israel (Exod. 1). Such hatred also occurred in Persia. As told in the book of Esther, hatred began simply with Haman's resentment of Mordecai. Soon the hatred grew, and Mordecai inspired the passage of a law to decimate all the Jews living in the Persian kingdom. Only an intervention of God through Esther the Queen spared the Jews. In Daniel's book, we are also told that 120 satraps sought to take Daniel's life because of his integrity. Daniel became one of three princes asked to supervise the satraps, limiting their ability to practice their pilfering against the king. So, they schemed until they got Daniel thrown into the lion's den. Of course, God spared Daniel until the king commanded that he be taken out of the den.

Many other examples could be cited, but the point of interest is to state that those who stand up for God will not be counted as friends of the world. Jesus told His disciples thus, "You will be hated … because of me" (Matt. 10:22; Mark 13:13). In fact, in John's gospel (John 15:18–25), Jesus gave at least five reasons why the world hates the children of God. (1) The world will hate God's children because it hated Christ first. (2) It will hate the children of God because they do not belong to the world. (3) It will hate the children of God because Christ has chosen them out of the world. (4) It will hate the children of God because it does not know the Father, who sent the Son into the world to save it. (5) It will hate for no good reason at all. They hate the children of God because the children of God are different.

Yes, the devil is always trying to stir up hatred everywhere.

> He makes people jealous of each other.
> He finds occasions to accuse the saints of God.
> He lays out schemes of trouble against people of character. He likes to ridicule those who stand up for truth.
> He constantly creates confusion in families—brothers against brothers, and sisters against sisters, and so on.
> He finds ways of turning friends into enemies.
> He turns ethnic communities against each other, creating racial and ethno-phobias.
> He seeks to sow the seeds of discord everywhere.
> He likes to hurt those who are seeking to extend the kingdom of God.
> He hates anything called forgiveness and reconciliation.
> He maintains an evil desire to murder anyone who stands for truth and righteousness.

Think about what I have said, in light of the following statement: "While hatred is cherished in the soul there is not one iota of the love of God there" (Ellen G. White, *Our High Calling*, p. 235). This is why the apostle Paul says:

> Bless those who persecute you; bless and do not curse. Rejoice with those who rejoice, and weep with those who weep. Be of the same mind toward one another. Do not set your mind on high things, but associate with the humble. Do not be wise in your own opinion. Repay no one evil for evil. Have regard for good things in the sight of all men. If it is possible, as much as depends on you, live peaceably with all men. Beloved, do not avenge yourselves, but rather give place to wrath; for it is written, "Vengeance is Mine, I will repay," says the Lord. Therefore: 'If your enemy is hungry, feed him; If he is thirsty, give him a drink; For in so doing you will heap coals of fire on his head.' Do not be overcome by evil, but overcome evil with good. (Rom. 12:14–21, NKJV)

Take a Moment

Write down the blessing that the above reading has brought to your mind today and for which you would wish to thank the Lord.

_____
_____
_____
_____
_____

Further, write down a special blessing that you would wish to ask the Lord to give you.

_____
_____
_____
_____
_____

Then, write down how and with whom you would wish to share your blessing.

_____
_____
_____
_____
_____

The Blessing of Being in God's Presence

And behold, the LORD stood above it [the ladder] and said: "I am the LORD God of Abraham your father and the God of Isaac; the land on which you lie I will give to you and your descendants. Also, your descendants shall be as the dust of the earth; you shall spread abroad to the west and the east, to the north and the south; and in you and your seed all the families of the earth shall be blessed. Behold, I am with you and will keep you wherever you go, and will bring you back to this land; for I will not leave you until I have done what I have spoken to you." Then Jacob awoke from his sleep and said, "Surely the LORD is in this place, and I did not know it." And he was afraid and said, "How awesome is this place! This is none other than the house of God, and this is the gate of heaven!" (Gen. 28:13–17, NKJV)

> When our prayers go up, God's blessings come down. When God's blessings come down, we are still to send our prayers up. Give thanks to God for every blessing. Our thankfulness opens the way for more blessings.

25.

The Blessing of Being in God's Presence

I grew up in a rural community where there was no electricity. For whatever reason, my mother would forget something that was needed for breakfast the next morning. Late in the afternoon, she would remember and send me to the store to get it. Before I could get back, it would be dark. While I was waiting on the shop keeper to serve me, idle men would be sitting in the piazza, telling ghost stories. Although I was taught that the dead could do no harm and, therefore, that I should not fear ghosts, my return journey home often made me feel a depth of fear. To deal with my fear I would often hum a comforting Christian song we were taught. The song made me feel the closeness of the divine presence.

Here I am reminded of Jacob as he journeyed to his uncle's house in Padan Aram, about 600 miles from home. It was one of those dark nights, and his fear was high. His conscience was heavy upon him. He knew that through deception, he had received the blessing that was intended for his brother Esau. He was struggling with his fear of Esau's rage. He was not sure whether Esau was following him to take his life. All he could see were the stars. But exhausted, he was forced to lie down to sleep. He took a stone to make a pillow and laid down. During the night, he had a most awesome dream. In the dream, he saw a ladder stretching from heaven to earth, with angels of God moving up and down on the ladder. The heart of the story is recorded in Genesis 28.

> And behold, the LORD stood above it [the ladder] and said: "I am the LORD God of Abraham your father and the God of Isaac; the land on which you lie I will give to you and your descendants. Also your descendants shall be as the dust of the earth; you shall spread abroad to the west and the east, to the north and the south; and in you and in your seed all the families of the earth shall be blessed. Behold, I am with you and will keep you wherever you go, and will bring you back to this land; for I will not leave you until I have done what I have spoken to you." (Gen. 28:13–15, NKJV)

Have you ever had a sweet dream? Jacob had one. He sensed that he was in the presence of God. As we read in the story:

> Then Jacob awoke from his sleep and said, "Surely the Lord is in this place, and I did not know it." And he was afraid and said, "How awesome is this place! This is none other than the house of God, and this is the gate of heaven!" (Gen. 28:16, 17, NKJV)

It makes a significant difference when one senses the presence of God in a dream or in any place, whether one is taking a journey or whether one is just at home. If God is present, it is heaven there. A song we sang often in the rise of the Jesus' movement in the late 1960s and early 1970s proclaims:

O what a wonderful, wonderful day
Day I will never forget.
After I'd wandered in darkness away
Jesus my Savior, I met.
O what a tender, compassionate friend;

He met the need of my heart.
Shadows dispelling, with joy I am telling
He made all the darkness depart.
Heaven came down and glory filled my soul (filled my soul).
When at the cross my Savior made me whole (made me whole).
My sins were washed away
And my night was turned to day.
Heaven came down and glory filled my soul.

Yes, when the presence of God is in a place there is awesomeness instead of awfulness. There is light in place of darkness. There is peace in place of conflict. There is love in place of hatred. There is purity in place of perversion. There is reverence and respect in place of insolence. There is comfort in place of anxiety. There is a call to worship instead abomination.

When we meet the harshest conditions, we need to pray for the presence of God, for only fools go where God is not. When God told Moses that he should go forward, but, because Israel was so rebellious, God would not go with them, Moses said to God "we cannot go if you will not go with us" (Exod. 33:15, paraphrase). Then who are we when we seek to go without God's presence?

Take a Moment

Write down the blessing that the above reading has brought to your mind today and for which you would wish to thank the Lord.

_____
_____
_____
_____
_____
_____

Further, write down a special blessing that you would wish to ask the Lord to give you.

_____
_____
_____
_____
_____
_____

Then, write down how and with whom you would wish to share your blessing.

_____
_____
_____
_____
_____
_____

Blessings for Barren Women

But Sarai was barren; she had no child. (Gen. 11:30, NKJV)

Now Sarai, Abram's wife, had borne him no children. (Gen. 16:1, NKJV)

Now Abraham and Sarah were old, well advanced in age; and Sarah had passed the age of childbearing. (Gen. 18:11, 12, NKJV)

> People may do everything right, thinking that life will offer them many blessings, but become frustrated because they don't get what they expected. However, later they find that what they considered a curse was actually a blessing. As Mark Batterson says, "Some of God's greatest blessings, are blessings in disguise."

26.

Blessings for Barren Women

When technological developments have made it possible for pregnancies to begin in so many different ways, much thought has not been given to the fact that being without a child is still one of the most significant challenges that many women continue to face psychologically, socially, culturally, and, at times, spiritually. But as I have listened to the testimonies of women who greatly desire to have children, who are considered barren, their stories have filled my heart with grief. It is not just what they feel about themselves, but how they are treated by the societies in which they live. A middle-aged woman, from an East African country, visited my church and testified on her frustration of childlessness. She asked us to pray for her, for, in her country, women who are barren are ridiculed, stigmatized, abused, and excluded from social groups in which they wish to participate. To deal with her pain, the woman said she had to form a support group.

Yes, it is awfully hard for many women to deal with the condition of barrenness. While many women have chosen to abort their pregnancies, it is noted that between 70 to 80 million of the world's population are infertile. It does not seem fair when so many women have chosen to abort that there are so many women with infertility. What blessing can there ever be in infertility?

Let us see if we can find some answers to the question by asking Rachel, that biblical character who struggled with her sister Leah. Leah was extremely fruitful, and Rachel was not.

Rachel was the woman Jacob loved, but, because of common customs and the cunning of Laban, Jacob's father-in-law, Leah was forced upon Jacob as a first wife. In all, Jacob had to wait fourteen years before he could marry Rachel, and he had to wait many more years before she would bring him a child. Since Leah gave Jacob many children, her position, as a wife, was dominant. And as Rachel felt despised, she became desperate. The tension between the two sisters vexed the soul of Jacob.

Thankfully, like the stories of Jacob's grandmother, Sarah, and his mother, Rebekah, the story of Rachel did not end with barrenness. She conceived and gave birth to two sons. The first son, Joseph, became one of Egypt's greatest governors and a savior figure for his father, for his brothers, and for their families. The second son, Ben-oni, or Benjamin, the "son of pain," cost Rachel her life. It is of interest that this son became quite respectable among the tribes in Israel, producing the first king of Israel (1 Sam. 9:15–27); the great warrior judge Ehud (Judges 3:12–30); Mordecai and Esther, who delivered Israel from the Persian genocide (Esther 2:5–7); and the great apostle Paul (Rom. 11:1; Phil. 3:5).

In fact, while Rachel did not live to witness most of the blessings upon her two sons and their children, she had an even more mysterious place in the history of Israel because, in the prophecy of Jeremiah 31:15, which is used in Matthew 2:16–18, she is presented in poetic language as "weeping … for her children and refusing to be comforted" (Jer. 31:15, NIV) until they are released from exile and restored to the land of promise.

What more general blessings are in Rachel's barrenness is not easy to state. What is obvious is that the barrenness created the anxiety, emptiness, loneliness, frustrations, grief, and other negative feelings that attend many barren women. Still, I want to help anyone facing stress of barrenness to find meaning in their most negative situation. Being a father of three sons, I cannot pretend to know totally what to say on these issues. However, here are some general ideas I have gathered about what barrenness teaches:

1. The development of patience and endurance during the time of waiting
2. A heightened appreciation for conception after a long time of barrenness
3. Persistence to keep trying in the face of ridicule and frustrations
4. The opportunity to surrender to the will of God
5. An opportunity to reflect more deeply on the meaning of pain
6. That we sometimes struggle in prayer to understand what God is trying to say in barrenness
7. That we can hold onto the promises of God despite our frustrations
8. The privilege of adopting and caring for children that are not of one's own birthing
9. That a person does not need to have a child in order to love and support parents and their children

10. That there is opportunity of being motherly regardless of not having children
11. That barrenness gives opportunity for the scientific development of fertility agents
12. That there is opportunity not to worry about children during times of distress.

Yes, barrenness can be a blessing in disguise. Jesus said, "For behold, the days are coming when they will say, 'Blessed are the barren, and the wombs that never bore, and the breasts that never nursed" (Luke 23:29, NASB 1977). Not that Jesus was against child bearing, but He knew of a distressing time that was to come when Titus would besiege Jerusalem, and mothers would be hungry, to the extent that many would even eat their own children to stay alive. So, He projected that, at such a time, women who had no children would be considered blessed.

Connected to what he saw as a time of distress, the prophet Isaiah brought comfort to Israel concerning a day of restoration when it would be said:

> Sing, O barren, you who have not borne! Break forth into singing, and cry aloud, you who have not labored with child! For more are the children of the desolate than the children of the married woman's children," says the LORD. "Enlarge the place of your tent, and let them stretch out the curtains of your dwellings; do not spare; lengthen your cords, and strengthen your stakes. For you shall expand to the right and to the left, and your descendants will inherit the nations, and make the desolate cities inhabited. Do not fear, for you will not be ashamed; neither be disgraced, for you will not be put to shame; for you will forget the shame of your youth, and will not remember the reproach of your widowhood anymore. For your Maker is your husband, the LORD of hosts is His name; and your Redeemer is the Holy One of Israel; He is called the God of the whole earth. For the LORD has called you like a woman forsaken and grieved in spirit, like a youthful wife when you were refused," says your God. (Isa. 54:1–6, NKJV)

There is no denying it that, though children are a blessing from the Lord and the fruit of the womb his reward (Ps. 127:3), having children does not fix every problem.

Women who have been denied the desired blessing of children have confessed that their barrenness has been a blessing in disguise. Thus, we conclude that there are many other ways in which blessings might come to a person other than through having children.

Take a Moment

Write down any blessing that the above reading has brought to your mind today and for which you would wish to thank the Lord.

_____
_____
_____
_____
_____
_____

Further, write down a special blessing that you would wish to ask the Lord to give you.

_____
_____
_____
_____
_____
_____

Then, write down how and with whom you would wish to share your blessing.

_____
_____
_____
_____
_____
_____

Wrestling for a Blessing

And he arose that night and took his two wives, his two female servants, and his eleven sons, and crossed over the ford of Jabbok. He took them, sent them over the brook, and sent over what he had. Then Jacob was left alone; and a Man wrestled with him until the breaking of day. Now when He saw that He did not prevail against him, He touched the socket of his hip; and the socket of Jacob's hip was out of joint as He wrestled with him. And He said, "Let Me go, for the day breaks." But he said, "I will not let You go unless You bless me!" So He said to him, "What is your name?" He said, "Jacob." And He said, "Your name shall no longer be called Jacob, but Israel; for you have struggled with God and with men, and have prevailed." Then Jacob asked, saying, "Tell me Your name, I pray." And He said, "Why is it that you ask about My name?" And He blessed him there. (Gen. 32:22–29, NKJV)

> We need to learn how to let go of our past and wrestle with God for our blessings. Jacob wrestled all night until he his thigh got hurt. Yet, in the end, his name was changed, and he became a different person.

27.
Wrestling for a Blessing

I know a judge who took the bar exams ten times before he was able to become an attorney. I have read of another person named Sam Goldstein who failed the bar eight times and is studying to take it again. His friends have advised him to give up and pursue another profession, but he's undeterred, especially after his latest attempt in which he came the closest to passing, falling short by just 13 points. I also know of a man who spent 40 days of fasting and praying to begin His ministry and just before His death spent a whole night in a garden struggling in prayer until He closed His prayer saying, "Father … not as I will but as you will" (Matt. 26:39, ESV).

The stories I just mentioned make me think of another man who spent a night wrestling with God at the ford of the Jabbok, a tributary of the Jordan River. It was the most significant struggle in his life. According to the story, after 21 years of slaving for his dishonest uncle who was also his father-in-law, he arose one night and stole away with his two wives, their two female servants, and his eleven sons and one daughter. When he came to the ford of the Jabbok, he sent his family and all he possessed across and stayed behind to prepare himself for meeting with his brother from whom he had stolen the birthright blessing. In the middle of the night, as he struggled in a dream, he was visited by a being that he thought to be his brother, so he engaged in a seeming fight to the death. After hours of struggle, the being touched him on his thigh, and Jacob realized that the being with whom he had been fighting was an angel visitor. So, he said, "I will not let You go unless You bless me" (Gen. 32:26, NKJV). After the Being revealed himself to Jacob, He blessed him. So, Jacob called the name of the place "Peniel," for, he said, "I have seen God face to face, and my life is preserved" (Gen. 32:30, KJV; you can read the full story in Genesis 32:22–29).

A major point in the story is that there are times and circumstances in which God's greatest blessings are made available. Those who are willing to wrestle are the ones who are most liable to receiving them. Jacob wrestled and received it. We might also state that often enough we become the greatest hindrance in blocking the blessings that God intends for us. We fail to exercise the faith, patience, or persistence that is required, and we come away empty from the moment of opportunity. Or, in more negative ways, we allow addictions (most of us have some), bad habits, negative attitudes, compulsive desires, lying, anger, temper, an unforgiving spirit, resentfulness, stubbornness, or laziness to block our way. Can we ever think that at any moment we are going to be successful without wrestling?

It is only those who are willing to deny self and agonize before God—only those who are willing to pray long and earnestly for God's blessings—who will obtain God's blessings. After the night of wrestling with God, Jacob became a different person. He was no longer a "deceiver" but a "victor"—a man of truth, of faith, and of love. He knew what it meant to find and frame a new life. He knew how to live a new life in God. At the end of the night's wrestling and victory, Jacob was so awed with the experience that he exclaimed, "I have seen the Lord." That was a powerful moment of insight, for from that moment on he became a different man. When a person sees the Lord, they will get a true understanding of who they are and will seek for a change. When the prophet Isaiah saw the Lord, he acknowledged who he was—a sinner living among other sinners. And having confessed and repented, the Lord offered him cleansing so that he could carry forward His mission (Isa. 6:1–6).

It is only those who are willing to deny self and agonize before God—only those who are willing to pray long and earnestly for God's blessings—who will obtain God's blessings.

What further lessons might we learn from Jacob and Isaiah, and from other biblical and extra-biblical characters about wrestling for God's blessings? As I have said before, there are forces in our world that are just waiting to block our way or steal away our blessings. Such forces are often within us. They might be our shadow selves. However, we can be victorious over them if we are prepared as the apostle Paul suggests—if we are ready to enter the battle and fight.

Put on the whole armor of God, that you may be able to stand against the wiles of the devil. 12 For we do not wrestle against flesh and blood, but against principalities, against powers, against the rulers of the darkness of this age, against spiritual hosts of wickedness in the heavenly places. 13 Therefore take up the whole armor of God, that you may be able to withstand in the evil day, and having done all, to stand. (Eph. 6:11–13, NKJV)

God is ever willing to give us His victorious blessings, but we must be ready to receive them. We must prepare for them and then act as if we have them. In our prayer life, we are to **A**sk for them, then **B**elieve that they are available, and then **C**laim them. These are the **ABC**s of prayer, through which we show that we are ready to receive God's blessings.

Take a Moment

Write down any blessing for which you have had to wrestle, and for which you would wish to thank the Lord.

_____
_____
_____
_____
_____
_____

Further, write down a special blessing that you would wish to ask the Lord to give you.

_____
_____
_____
_____
_____
_____

Then, write down how and with whom you would wish to share your blessing.

_____
_____
_____
_____
_____
_____

A Name Change for a Blessing

Then God appeared to Jacob again, when he came from Padan Aram, and blessed him. And God said to him, "Your name is Jacob; your name shall not be called Jacob anymore, but Israel shall be your name." So He called his name Israel. Also God said to him: "I am God Almighty. Be fruitful and multiply; a nation and a company of nations shall proceed from you, and kings shall come from your body. The land which I gave Abraham and Isaac I give to you; and to your descendants after you I give this land." Then God went up from him in the place where He talked with him. So Jacob set up a pillar in the place where He talked with him, a pillar of stone; and he poured a drink offering on it, and he poured oil on it. And Jacob called the name of the place where God spoke with him, Bethel. (Gen. 35:9–15, NKJV)

> Our names influence our lives. Some parents do not realize how much they impact their children by the names that they have chosen to give them. Just imagine how Benjamin would have felt if he were to live by the name "Benoni," which means "Son of my sorrow," as his mother had given him. That is why his father Jacob changed his name to "Benjamin," which means "son of my right hand." Jacob would shortly learn the true significance of his own name change.

28.

A Name Change for a Blessing

When was the last time that you took a moment to reflect on the meaning of your name or the name of a person you might know? The 45th president of the United States is known for his genius in naming—or branding—things or people. In his race for the presidency, he found names for every one of his opponents, and it seemed, somehow, that he was able to impact people's public perceptions regarding most of the people to whom he gave a name. The names that he called his opponents were pejorative, but many around him accepted his uncanny ability as distinctive of his negotiating power. He continued the "branding" throughout his presidency, using the strategy against foreign leaders, and it seemed to have gotten some who were intimidated to negotiate with him. It is not pleasant to be called names that are pejorative, uncivil or uncouth, or names you just do not like. There is something quite fascinating about the human attempt to name things and people, which often suggests rebellion, but I leave this observation to another discussion.

What is of interest here is that, when God wants to create a new identity for a person, he has to name (or rename) them. Let us observe how it was done in the life of Jacob.

> Then God appeared to Jacob again, when he came from Padan Aram, and blessed him. And God said to him, "Your name is Jacob; your name shall not be called Jacob anymore, but Israel shall be your name." So, He called his name Israel. Also God said to him: "I am God Almighty. Be fruitful and multiply; a nation and a company of nations shall proceed from you, and kings shall come from your body. The land which I gave Abraham and Isaac I give to you; and to your descendants after you I give this land." Then God went up from him in the place where He talked with him. So Jacob set up a pillar in the place where He talked with him, a pillar of stone; and he poured a drink offering on it, and he poured oil on it. And Jacob

called the name of the place where God spoke with him, Bethel. (Gen. 35:9–15, NKJV)

What a transformation! After a night of wrestling with God, Jacob was given a new name. He was called "Israel." Before this he was Jacob "the supplanter," Jacob "the heal grabber," Jacob "the deceiver," Jacob "the cheater." But after the night of encounter with God, he came away with the name of "Israel." A close analysis of the Hebrew *Yisra-el* shows that it means "God contends." He is changed from Jacob to Israel "the God-striver," Israel "the overcomer," Israel "the victor." He needed a new identity and he received it. God adopted him and gave him a new name. Just like Abram "the exiled father," who became Abraham the "exalted father," "the father of nations," so Jacob was "chosen" by God to be the father of "the chosen people." Jacob was transformed. He could have been killed in the night of wrestling with God, but, in mercy, God saved him, and renamed him, setting him on a new path.

With the name change, Jacob stepped into a new, more intimate relationship with God. Just as a woman who enters the marital relationship changes her name, God changed Jacob's name, creating for him a new identity. Likewise in an adoption, the adopted one takes on the new family name and becomes one with the family. Israel, the progeny of Jacob, God's chosen, as a corporate community would be referenced as God's "virgin" (Lamentations 2:13), His "bride" (Rev. 21:2), or His "wife" (Hosea 2:2), and as God's "son," His "firstborn" (Exod. 4:23; Jer. 31:9), His "inheritance," His "possession" (Deut. 32:9), His "people" (Exod. 34). Yes, in the naming, as God did for Jacob, there is profound significance. The followers of Christ are called "sons and daughters" of God (2 Cor. 6:18). Through the process of spiritual adoption (Rom. 8:15), we enter into the family of God. Our names are changed. We are rebranded; we are His adopted children.

Understanding the ways in which names are misconstrued in this world, where humanity wants to take over the prerogative of God to attach to others a name, one can see why, in the book of Revelation, those who overcome will each be given a new name. "The one who conquers, I will make him a pillar in the temple of my God. Never shall he go out of it, and I will write on him the name of my God, and the name of the city of my God, the new Jerusalem, which comes down from my God out of heaven, and my own new name" (Rev. 3:12, ESV). "Then I looked, and behold, on Mount Zion stood the Lamb, and with him 144,000 who had his name and his Father's name written on their foreheads" (Rev. 14:1, ESV). Until the end, the name given will remain a mystery except to the one who receives it (Rev. 2:17).

Yes, when God sees His children with the names that He has given to them, He will take them into His Kingdom. Thus, my conclusion is that, if you have a name that you do not like, don't worry, it is only a place holder. When you are adopted into the family of God, you will receive a blessed name—*Yisra-el*—"Overcomer"—and such a name will be good enough that you will find your place in the kingdom of God.

Take a Moment

Write down the blessing that the above reading has brought to your mind today and for which you would wish to thank the Lord.

_____
_____
_____
_____
_____
_____

Further, write down a special blessing that you would wish to ask the Lord to give you.

_____
_____
_____
_____
_____
_____

Then, write down how and with whom you would wish to share your blessing.

_____
_____
_____
_____
_____
_____

A Name Change for a Blessing

A Blessed Destiny

Then Jacob said to Simeon and Levi, "You have troubled me by making me obnoxious among the inhabitants of the land, among the Canaanites and the Perizzites; and since I am few in number, they will gather themselves together against me and kill me. I shall be destroyed, my household and I." (Gen. 34:30, NKJV)

By the God of your father who will help you, and by the Almighty who will bless you with blessings of heaven above, blessings of the deep that lies beneath, blessings of the breasts and of the womb. The blessings of your father have excelled the blessings of my ancestors, up to the utmost bound of the everlasting hills. They shall be on the head of Joseph, and on the crown of the head of him who was separate from his brothers.... All these are the twelve tribes of Israel, and this is what their father spoke to them. And he blessed them; he blessed each one according to his own blessing. (Gen. 49:25, 26, 28, NKJV)

> We are never to forget that a blessing can be decisive, as it settles an issue and produces its result. As a spouse, a parent, a friend, a leader, or a teacher, can you let go of your past with all your insecurities to bless those around you?

29.

A Blessed Destiny

After surveying the series of blessings in the book of Genesis, it is profoundly exciting to come to the last words of blessing that Jacob laid upon his sons. Some people have called the whole episode, "The Blessing of Jacob." To me, much of what is said does not seem like the last words of blessings, for there are also curses. Jacob was facing the final moments of his life on earth, and wished, for the last time, to speak the truth into his sons' ears. The record of the words in Genesis 49 is rather explicit, and we who seek to pass on blessings might learn a lot from reading them. What does a person say to those standing by him or her at death, those who are expected to carry on their dreams, ideas, and plans? Is their time for political correctness? or is it time to tell the truth?

Commentator Matthew Henry offers some thoughts on the manner in which Jacob spoke to his sons. I paraphrase what he says, as follows. While Jacob was on his deathbed, making his will, he was able to express what he found hard to say until his final moments. A dying man, his words carried a heavy weight. They would be remembered for a long time. What he said then he feared to say when he was in his full strength. But in his moment of greatest vulnerability, the Spirit chose to give him liberty. Thus, he declared what God intended for each son in the future. His words were not just words to his sons but were also focused on the twelve tribes of Israel, which were to occupy Canaan as the land of their inheritance.

As his sons sensed the prospect of his death, they listened with intensity. Jacob did not hide what he thought of each son. He stated why Ruben lost his place as the leader in the family. Ruben had allowed his passion to control him, so that he had sexual intercourse with one of Jacob's wives. Then he rebuked Simeon and Levi for their uncontrollable anger and cruelty. He was displeased for what they had done to Hamor and his sons in revenge for Shechem's raping of their sister Dinah. Remember the words of Jacob to Simeon and Levi, "You've made my name stink to high heaven among the people here, these Canaanites and Perizzites. If they decided to gang up on us and attack, as few as we are we wouldn't stand a chance; they'd wipe my people and me right off the map" (Gen. 34:30, *The Message*). To Issachar, Zebulun, Gad, Dan, Benjamin, Asher and Naphtali, Jacob offered qualified blessings. Then he lingered long on Judah and Joseph, the two sons who would establish the largest part of the inheritance blessings in the future of Israel. Judah would become the progenitor of David and of Jesus, the Messiah, while Ephraim, the youngest son of Joseph, would become the corporate head of the ten tribes of Israel. Six times in his prophecy about Joseph, Jacob spoke of the sources of Joseph's blessings:

> And by the Almighty who will bless you with blessings of heaven above,
> Blessings of the deep that lies beneath,
> Blessings of the breasts and of the womb.
> The blessings of your father
> Have excelled the blessings of my ancestors,
> Up to the utmost bound of the everlasting hills.
> They shall be on the head of Joseph,
> And on the crown of the head of him who was separate from his brothers (Gen. 49:25, 26, NKJV).

Every blessing was prophetic, though not pre-determinative because Levi, for example, would change the course of his history when his descendants stood against the apostasy of Israel on their journey to Canaan from Egypt. The only way that each of the sons and their posterity could obtain blessings or avoid curses was to live in harmony with the promises of the covenant. Notice what the editor said at the end of the dispensing of the blessings, "All these are the twelve tribes of Israel: and this is it that their father spake unto them, and blessed them; every one according to his blessing he blessed them" (Gen. 49:28, KJV).

The conclusion of the reflection seeks to remind us that a father or mother might have some great insights into a child's future. Their insights do not ultimately determine the direction the child will go, but they will help a wise child to take precautions. Only God determines a destiny, and anyone who will cooperate with God will be able to have a right destiny. The Psalmist reminds us of the path of the righteous over against the path of the wicked by noting that, while the righteous seek the path of the "blessed," the wicked stand and linger in the path of the wicked. "Therefore the wicked shall not stand in the judgment, nor sinners in the congregation of the righteous" (Ps. 1:5, ASV).

Take a Moment

Write down the blessing that the above reading has brought to your mind today and for which you would wish to thank the Lord.

_____
_____
_____
_____
_____
_____

Further, write down a special blessing that you would wish to ask the Lord to give you.

_____
_____
_____
_____
_____
_____

Then, write down how and with whom you would wish to share your blessing.

_____
_____
_____
_____
_____
_____

Generational Blessings

Then Israel saw Joseph's sons, and said, "Who are these?"

Joseph said to his father, "They are my sons, whom God has given me in this place."

And he said, "Please bring them to me, and I will bless them." Now the eyes of Israel were dim with age so, that he could not see. Then Joseph brought them near him, and he kissed them and embraced them. And Israel said to Joseph, "I had not thought to see your face; but in fact, God has also shown me your offspring!"

So Joseph brought them from beside his knees, and he bowed down with his face to the earth. And Joseph took them both, Ephraim with his right hand toward Israel's left hand, and Manasseh with his left hand toward Israel's right hand, and brought them near him. Then Israel stretched out his right hand and laid it on Ephraim's head, who was the younger, and his left hand on Manasseh's head, guiding his hands knowingly, for Manasseh was the firstborn. And he blessed Joseph, and said:

"God, before whom my fathers Abraham and Isaac walked, The God who has fed me all my life long to this day, The Angel who has redeemed me from all evil, Bless the lads; Let my name be named upon them, And the name of my fathers, Abraham and Isaac; And let them grow into a multitude in the midst of the earth." (Gen. 48:8–16, NKJV)

> When you offer a blessing to another generation, you have begun a wave that will expand into a flood. Let it flow! Someone will benefit from it.

30.

Generational Blessings

I am the fifth child in my family. Five more came after me. This makes me truly engrossed when I hear a discussion on birth order and its impact on people's personalities, IQ, character traits, relationships, and other matters that are evident in people's lives. Some individuals even talk about the blessings that come to their first children. I have never argued or have wished to argue with anyone I hear discussing the influence of birth order, but I have had a deep haunt that there are lots of things in the dynamics of childbearing and rearing that might trash some of the logic about the blessings based on birth order.

Let me point to something that I have noticed as I have read the life of Joseph: it is noted that birth order does not necessarily determine the path to one's blessing. The path seems like a cycle, for it was the same with Isaac and Ishmael, Jacob and Esau, Joseph and his brothers, and Joseph's two sons—Manasseh and Ephraim. The whole story is told in Genesis 48. The background of the story is that Jacob had become old, quite weak, and dim of eye. A close reading of the text might suggest that he might have been also a little hard of hearing. Jacob was soon to die, so Joseph took his two sons to visit him on his bedside. Upon hearing that Joseph had come to visit, Jacob gathered his strength and sat up. He took the time to recite how God had blessed him on his pilgrimage over the years. Those who know the way that Jacob spoke will likely notice that there was no note of self-pity. All he did was bless God for making his life "fruitful." Then he claimed Joseph's two sons, who were born in Egypt, as his own sons. This claim meant that they would inherit the covenant blessings like the rest of his sons.

A fascinating part of the story, of course, is how Jacob identified the presence of Joseph's sons, Manasseh and Ephraim. After their identification, Jacob embraced and kissed them. Then it was the time for the blessing. Joseph took Manasseh, as the firstborn, in his right and Ephraim in his left hand. He expected Jacob to pass the blessing of the firstborn to Manasseh, and Ephraim the lesser portion of the blessing. But Jacob crossed his hands as he offered the blessing. Joseph sought to correct Jacob by fixing Jacob's hands as he thought they should be, but Jacob re-crossed his hands and placed them, as he wished them to be. Ephraim was to receive the greater blessing, while Manasseh was to receive the lesser blessing.

Don't say, "senile old man," or "stubborn old fellow," for Jacob was deep in reflection, if not a moment of prophetic revelation. He knew precisely what he was doing. He was declaring the future of Joseph's two sons. Ephraim would become more dominant in Israel. Ten tribes of Israel would be called "Ephraim." In the Scriptural tradition, the logic or pattern of blessing seems to be the same: Cain was Adam's firstborn, but Abel was the more blessed. Ishmael was Abraham's firstborn, but Isaac received the greater blessing. Esau was Isaac's firstborn, but Jacob received the greater blessing. Jacob also blessed Joseph. Even though Ruben was his firstborn, Jacob considered Joseph, the chief son of his inheritance. Of course, his blessing did not stop with Joseph, but was passed on to Joseph's two sons.

The fact of interest is that blessings do not follow ordinary human logic. They work according to the divine purpose of divine grace and one's willingness to cooperate with God.

Here are some lessons that might be extracted from the story:

1. It is not automatic that, because one is a firstborn, a person will lose his or her blessing. Blessings come from God and are distributed by God's grace. So, we can trust ourselves to God for our own particular blessing.
2. Don't assume that your blessings are automatic because you are in a privileged position as a first, second, third, fourth, or fifth-born child. Again, blessings are up to God to distribute, and, often enough, He guides the human agent to pass on the blessings as He wills.
3. Don't think that your fame or possessions provide the path to all your blessings.
4. Human logic is different from divine logic in the distribution of blessings.
5. Divine wisdom supersedes human wisdom in the giving and receiving of blessings.
6. Human beings look at the outward appearance, but God looks at the heart.

7. The blessings that are the most significant focus of life are not the material possessions or the successes in this life but the blessings of our eternal destiny.

The question that confronts each of us is whether we are willing to open ourselves to the destiny that God has chosen or whether we are inclined to insist on our own way. If we accept God's sovereign freedom, we will humble our hearts to receive the blessings. If we resist, we will lose all that is in store for us.

> *The question that confronts each of us is whether we are willing to open ourselves to the destiny that God has chosen or whether we are inclined to insist on our own way.*

Take a Moment

Write down the blessing that the above reading has brought to your mind today and for which you would wish to thank the Lord.

_____
_____
_____
_____
_____
_____

Further, write down a special blessing that you would wish to ask the Lord to give you.

_____
_____
_____
_____
_____
_____

Then, write down how and with whom you would wish to share your blessing.

_____
_____
_____
_____
_____
_____

The Blessings of Dreaming

"Here we were, binding sheaves in the field. Then behold, my sheaf arose and also stood upright; and indeed, your sheaves stood all around and bowed down to my sheaf."

And his brothers said to him, "Shall you indeed reign over us? Or shall you indeed have dominion over us?" So, they hated him even more for his dreams and for his words.

Then he dreamed still another dream and told it to his brothers, and said, "Look, I have dreamed another dream. And this time, the sun, the moon, and the eleven stars bowed down to me."

So he told it to his father and his brothers; and his father rebuked him and said to him, "What is this dream that you have dreamed? Shall your mother and I and your brothers indeed come to bow down to the earth before you?" (Gen. 37:7–10, NKJV)

> Your dream might be a blessing in disguise. Seek to understand your dream and act on it.

31.

The Blessings of Dreaming

Those of us who live in the United States of America say that we live in a land for dreamers. People come to the United States from everywhere to realize "the American dream." Many have found, of course, that instead of the realization of the dream, they find a nightmare. But dreams can have positive as well as negative outcomes. On the one hand, while dreaming can focus the mind on positive goals and bring about success, dreaming can also be merely fictional ideas, false imaginations, idle contemplations, fabricated projections, and wild thoughts that are not grounded in reality. The latter can be of such magnitude that they twist the personality and misdirect the behavior of an individual until he or she is destroyed.

This being said, let me follow the story of a dreamer whose dreams got him into trouble, though he had a powerful outcome. Successful people know that their dreams can get them into trouble before they get the positive outcome. The dreamer in our story is Joseph.

We know where the dreams of Joseph led him. At certain moments, he might have asked whether he was dreaming or just having nightmares. He had a dream and recounted it to his brothers, and immediately he could tell that they were not very happy. He told them, "We were binding sheaves of grain out in the field when suddenly my sheaf rose and stood upright, while your sheaves gathered around mine and bowed down to it" (Gen. 37:7, NIV). Do you blame the brothers for getting angry? Imagine the eleventh child in the family suggesting that he would "rule" over his brothers. He had a second dream and recounted it to the brothers, "Listen," ... "I had another dream, and this time the sun and moon and eleven stars were bowing down to me" (Gen. 37:9, NIV). When his father heard the dream, his father rebuked him, saying, "What is this dream you had? Will your mother and I and your brothers actually come and bow down to the ground before you?" (Gen. 37:10). While the brothers became profoundly jealous of Joseph, "his father kept the matter in mind."

The brothers had to go far away from home to care for their sheep. After a while, Jacob, not knowing the anger of the brothers, sent Joseph to visit them and see how they were doing. As soon as the brothers saw Joseph approaching at a distance, they said to one another, "Here comes this dreamer. Come now, let us kill him and throw him into one of the pits; then we shall say that a wild animal has devoured him, and we shall see what will become of his dreams" (Gen. 37:19, NRSV).

So, the rest of the story continues as the brothers took Joseph and threw him into a pit. Then, after a while, they saw some Midianite traders (descendants of Ishmael) passing by, and they took him out of the pit and sold him to them for twenty pieces of silver. The slave traders took him to Egypt and sold him on the "auction block." He ended up a servant in the house of one Potiphar, where he served so well that he became the head steward of the house. As the story goes, from the time he first entered the house, Potiphar's wife set her eyes on him. One day, when Joseph was at home with her alone, Potiphar's wife made sexual advances toward him. He would not accept her advances, and she grabbed at him. He ran away as quickly as he could, leaving his outer garment in her hands. She failed in her object but decided to frame him. As soon as Potiphar came home, she showed him the clothes and gave him her story. While Potiphar, likely did not believe her, he put Joseph in prison. Some commentators have suggested that the prison was a pit. After he had been in prison for some time, two of his prison mates, namely the butler and baker of Pharaoh, had dreams. He was able to interpret the dreams. And the dreams came through exactly as he had interpreted them. Later, when Pharaoh had his dreams and needed an interpreter, the butler who was reinstated to his post, as Joseph had said, told Pharaoh about Joseph, and Pharaoh called him to his court. Joseph offered clear interpretations of Pharaoh's dreams, predicting seven years of plenty followed by seven years of famine. Pharaoh could see that there was something special about Joseph. In thinking of someone who could carry out his dreams, preparing for the famine, Pharaoh chose Joseph to be the chief administrator of his kingdom.

Our overall deduction is that, since dreams can serve to inspire and motivate us, we need to dream. But as we dream, we are to make sure that God is at the center of each dream. Even though our dreams may take us through some time of trouble, when God inspires our dreams, He will guide us to the greatest fulfillment of our dreams.

Take a Moment

Write down the blessing that the above reading has brought to your mind today and for which you would wish to thank the Lord.

_____
_____
_____
_____
_____
_____

Further, write down a special blessing that you would wish to ask the Lord to give you.

_____
_____
_____
_____
_____
_____

Then, write down how and with whom you would wish to share your blessing.

_____
_____
_____
_____
_____
_____

The Blessings of Self-Control

Then Joseph could no longer control himself before all his attendants, and he cried out, "Have everyone leave my presence!" So there was no one with Joseph when he made himself known to his brothers. (Gen. 45:1, NIV)

> Whether or not you are a firstborn, never forget that you are privileged to receive God's blessings. And after you receive them, never forget that there is someone waiting for you to share them with.

32.

The Blessings of Self-Control

We are in a time in our land when anger, resentment, rage, and vengefulness are being used to gain political advantage and being held up as great virtues. Here we need to do some reflection on their negative and destructive power by focusing on the need for self-control. Self-control is of great importance, especially when we hear so much name-calling, efforts at so-called branding, belittling, misrepresentation, and other pejoratives in our common discourse. It is my view that anyone who does not admit to the destructive power of the lack of self-control must be oblivious to its negative consequence in the history of humanity. Yes, it is true that, while today's politicians might be making use of a lack of self-control to win elections in the short term, it needs to be made clear that, in the long term, the devil is having a field day and is stoking the fires of hell that will not be easily put out. The point is that, if we cannot learn self-control, we are open to conflicts and self-destruction.

In reading the story of Joseph and his encounter with Madam Potiphar, it is admirable to see how he was able to be victorious because of his self-control. Mrs. Potiphar used all her seductive powers to entrap Joseph, but Joseph was able to get away from her. He had to fight his way to victory. He had to leave his coat in her hands as he was running away, and she used it to frame him and land him in prison. However, through it all, he maintained his integrity.

What a great lesson in self-control! It was not something that happened in an instant. Self-control is one of the first and primary virtues any person must exercise if he or she is to be successful. If it is to be seated in a person in a most effective way, self-control needs to be taught to the person from childhood. However it came to Joseph, it is evident that he learned it well. He knew how to guard his passions and emotions, focus on the divine purpose and destiny, work with the divine plan, respect boundaries, stay away from extremes and keep the balance in his life, control his thoughts and speech, and take the right action. He learned to think before he acted. He had a real sense of what is meant by self-control.

> *Only with self-denial and submission to the power that is beyond us can we take control of that which is within us.*

An observation needs to be made that self-control does not mean that one is dependent on oneself. It does not mean an unwillingness to take counsel or to cast aside wisdom and instruction. Rather, it means that one is putting oneself under divine control. Only with self-denial and submission to the power that is beyond us can we take control of that which is within us. Those who are given to self-trust have often found that when they face a crisis, they fail. This is why one is advised not to put oneself into situations of temptation with the expectation that one will be able to have enough personal resources to protect oneself. Peter advises: "Be alert and of sober mind. Your enemy the devil prowls around like a roaring lion looking for someone to devour" (1 Peter 5:8, NIV).

The writer of the Proverbs also advises:

> Do not enter the path of the wicked, and do not walk in the way of evil. Avoid it, do not travel on it; turn away from it and pass on. (Prov. 4:14, 15, NKJV)

In exercising self-control and gaining the victory over seduction, it might seem that things did not turn out for Joseph that well, for, instead of getting an immediate promotion to be chief administrator of Egypt, he landed up in prison. Yet, though he was in prison, he was not struggling with guilt or shame or regrets. He knew that God knew the truth about him.

God blessed him by overruling his situation, by allowing him to be let out of jail to become the governor of Egypt. Then, in the providence of God, the great famine in Canaan forced his brothers to look for food in Egypt. Joseph was in a position to humiliate them if he wished. He could have unleashed his rage on them. When he saw them at first, it is likely that his anger burned within him. But he controlled himself. He refused to stand in judgment against them for what they had done to him. Although he tested them, he preserved their lives.

After revealing himself to them, it is said that he could no longer control himself in front of all his attendants. The writer of the story says that he cried out, " 'Have everyone leave my presence!' So, there was no one with Joseph when he made himself known to his brothers" (Gen. 45:1). Yes, he lost control of his emotions, but it was in expressing his joy in the forgiveness and reconciliation of his brothers.

Take a Moment

Write down the blessing that the above reading has brought to your mind today and for which you would wish to thank the Lord.

_____
_____
_____
_____
_____
_____

Further, write down a special blessing that you would wish to ask the Lord to give you in relation to self-control.

_____
_____
_____
_____
_____
_____

Then, write down how and with whom you would wish to share such a blessing.

_____
_____
_____
_____
_____
_____

The Blessings of Integrity

But it happened about this time when Joseph went into the house to do his work, and none of the men of the house was inside, that she caught him by his garment, saying, "Lie with me." But he left his garment in her hand, and fled and ran outside. And so it was, when she saw that he had left his garment in her hand and fled outside, that she called to the men of her house and spoke to them, saying, "See, he has brought in to us a Hebrew to mock us. He came in to me to lie with me, and I cried out with a loud voice. And it happened, when he heard that I lifted my voice and cried out, that he left his garment with me, and fled and went outside." So she kept his garment with her until his master came home. Then she spoke to him with words like these, saying, "The Hebrew servant whom you brought to us came in to me to mock me; so it happened, as I lifted my voice and cried out, that he left his garment with me and fled outside." So it was, when his master heard the words which his wife spoke to him, saying, "Your servant did to me after this manner," that his anger was aroused. Then Joseph's master took him and put him into the prison, a place where the king's prisoners were confined. And he was there in the prison. But the LORD was with Joseph and showed him mercy, and He gave him favor in the sight of the keeper of the prison. And the keeper of the prison committed to Joseph's hand all the prisoners who were in the prison; whatever they did there, it was his doing. The keeper of the prison did not look into anything that was under Joseph's authority, because the LORD was with him; and whatever he did, the LORD made it prosper. (Gen. 39:11–25, NKJV)

> The greatest treasure of life is one's integrity, and, when it is secure, it will be a blessing to many generations.

33.

The Blessings of Integrity

Have you ever been accused of anything you did not do? I have been accused, and do I need to tell you that it was not easy to keep my sanity? On one occasion, when I faced a false accusation, I prayed to God for grace. But for many nights I did not sleep—I kept thinking about how to stop the perpetrators of the rumors against me. One day, as I was standing at the door of our church shaking hands, my wife noticed that I was not dealing with the accusation in a healthy way. She came to stand beside me, and, after a brief moment, held onto my arm and said, "We are going now." She must have been surprised how easily I responded to her suggestion, for we left immediately. On reaching home, she held my arm again, and said, "We are going to the bedroom, now." Again, I followed her instructions without a word. On reaching the bedroom, she drew me beside the bed and dropped to her knees and said, "Let us pray." I cannot forget that day because it was truly transformational. My integrity was being challenged, and I was anxious and angry. But after the prayer, I felt peace.

Then I thought of Joseph and the lie that was told against him, which landed him in prison. The challenge to his integrity did not only start when he served in Potiphar's house; it started in his parental house when he shared his dreams with his brothers and father and drew his brothers' ire. We read, "Joseph reported to his father some of the bad things his brothers were doing" (Gen. 37:2, NLT). That was reason enough for them to hate him. His character contradicted theirs. And just as it would happen to Jesus, whose brothers hated Him for His integrity, so did it happen with Joseph. Thus, when Joseph went to visit his brothers in the field, where they were tending their sheep, they stripped off his robe and cast him into a pit. Then they took him out and sold him to slave traders passing by. The traders took him to Egypt and auctioned him as a slave. He became a servant in the house of Potiphar, who was the head military guard for Pharaoh. There, Joseph worked effectively and honestly, and Potiphar took notice. Soon Potiphar put him in charge of everything he owned.

From the day he came to work for Potiphar, Potiphar's wife set her eyes on Jacob, and she did all she could to seduce him. Yet, he kept his distance from her. One day when \\ Potiphar was out of the house, Mrs. Potiphar propositioned Joseph, and he told her, "NO!" This made Mrs. Potiphar so angry that she planted a lie on him. She told her husband, and he accepted her story and sent Joseph to prison, where he spent two years. During Joseph's time in prison, the chief of the prison noticed that he was a person of integrity and put him in charge of the prisoners. In prison, Joseph worked hard and was admired by all.

Then came the day when Pharaoh's butler and baker had dreams and asked Joseph to help them understand what their dreams meant. Joseph gave them interpretations that worked out precisely. In keeping with his dream, in three days the chief butler was restored to his place in the palace, while, in keeping with his dream, the chief baker was beheaded. Before the butler was taken out of prison, Joseph asked him to remember him to Pharaoh, and the butler assured him that he would, but he forgot.

About two years after the butler was restored, Pharaoh had two dreams, and none of his court magicians were able to give him their interpretation. Then it was that the butler remembered Joseph, and he brought him to the attention of Pharaoh. Pharaoh got extremely excited and sent for Joseph. Joseph was then "brought from the dungeon" and given a change of clothing. He was taken to Pharaoh and given the opportunity to interpret the Pharaoh's dreams. He stated that there would be seven years of abundance in the land of Egypt followed by seven years of famine. He then recommended that "a discerning and wise man" be put in charge of making preparations for the famine, namely, that food should be collected during the good years and stored for the years of famine (Gen. 41).

Before Pharaoh could commend Joseph and select the person to administer the project, Joseph made it clear that "the thing is established by God, and God will shortly bring it to pass" (Gen. 41:32, NKJV).

In effect, Joseph's integrity came through brightly. He did not take credit for the dreams' interpretation. He did not make it seem that he was the one for the project's administration. In response, the report states:

> And the thing was good in the eyes of Pharaoh, and in the eyes of all his servants. And Pharaoh said unto his servants, Can we find such a one as this is, a man in whom the Spirit of God is?

And Pharaoh said unto Joseph, Forasmuch as God hath showed thee all this, there is none so discreet and wise as thou art: Thou shalt be over my house, and according unto thy word shall all my people be ruled: only in the throne will I be greater than thou. And Pharaoh took off his ring from his hand, and put it upon Joseph's hand, and arrayed him in vestures of fine linen, and put a gold chain about his neck; and he made him to ride in the second chariot which he had; and they cried before him, Bow the knee: and he made him ruler over all the land of Egypt. And Pharaoh said unto Joseph, I am Pharaoh, and without thee shall no man lift up his hand or foot in all the land of Egypt. (Gen. 41:39–40, 42–44, KJV)

Need we say more about Joseph's integrity? What is of interest is that regardless of circumstances, he maintained his integrity. The point is that:

1. Integrity is not so much a question of one's reputation as it is of what is the center of one's character.
2. Integrity comes from daily discipline. It is not something that comes just at moments of testing.
3. Integrity means telling the truth in every situation.
4. Integrity means that principles take precedence over popularity.
5. Integrity leads a person to take responsibility for his or her actions.
6. Integrity means that morality is counted above monetary incentives.
7. Integrity may cause others to hate us and may put our lives in turmoil, but integrity stands out in difficult times.

What is most significant for a person of integrity is to know that there are mighty blessings that are the consequences of integrity. We can note, for example, the following blessings;

1. A person of integrity builds and preserves relationships (1 Cor. 8:12).
2. A person of integrity receives the favor of God (1 Chron. 29:17).
3. A person of integrity builds a lasting legacy. "A righteous person lives on the basis of his integrity. Blessed are his children after he is gone" (Prov. 20:7, GW).
4. A person of integrity is open to receiving the eternal rewards of God (Matt. 25:21).
5. A person of integrity is more prone to making right decisions.

6. A person of integrity is set apart from the multitude (Prov. 19:1).
7. A person of integrity has a positive influence on others (Luke 16:10).

Yes, you can count your blessings when you live a life of integrity. As the Proverbs declare: "A righteous person lives on the basis of his integrity. Blessed are his children after he is gone" (Prov. 20:7, GW).

Take a Moment

Write down the blessing that the above reading has brought to your mind today and for which you would wish to thank the Lord.

_____
_____
_____
_____
_____
_____

Further, write down a special blessing that you would wish to ask the Lord to give you.

_____
_____
_____
_____
_____
_____

Then, write down how and with whom you would wish to share your blessing.

_____
_____
_____
_____
_____
_____

The Blessings of Positive Living

So Joseph found favor in his sight, and served him. Then he made him overseer of his house, and all that he had he put under his authority. So it was, from the time that he had made him overseer of his house and all that he had, that the LORD blessed the Egyptian's house for Joseph's sake; and the blessing of the LORD was on all that he had in the house and in the field. Thus he left all that he had in Joseph's hand, and he did not know what he had except for the read which he ate. Now Joseph was handsome in form and appearance. (Gen. 39:4–6, NKJV)

> When I think of the phrase, "the Lord blessed the Egyptian's house for Joseph's sake," it gives me chills because it leads me to ask myself, *How many people have been blessed because of me?*

34.

The Blessings of Positive Living

Have you ever met anyone who complains all the time—a person who whines about everything, a person who grumbles and lashes out at everyone they meet? You stand around such people and you begin to feel anxious enough that you just want to get out of the bad air that swirls around them. They make a work environment so depressive that you feel stressed. They are so miserable that you fear getting close to them. They would make it seem that the troubles that they face are the worst in the world. They are just bitter. They do not have friends for they distrust everyone for the injuries that they have sustained.

Yes, I am sure you have met people like the ones I have questioned you described. In reviewing the life of Joseph, I have concluded that he could have been such a person. He had good reasons to feel as I have described. Without taking note of the positive moments in his life, he could rightly have catalogued—

1. How his brothers were jealous of him because of his dreams
2. How they put him in a pit, when he went to visit them to ascertain their safety and well-being.
3. How his brothers sold him into Egyptian slavery
4. How he was thrown in prison when he resisted the overtures of Mrs. Potiphar
5. How he was left in prison for two years, even though the butler assured him that he would let Pharaoh know of his situation when the butler was restored to his palace duties.

Yes, the path of Joseph's life to the governorship of Egypt was not strewn with roses. He had every reason to complain, whine, grumble, scold, and lash out under the difficult circumstances in which he found himself. But he did not do any such thing. We have no scriptural record of his giving attention to the negative thought that the devil might have introduced to his mind. What we read is that, because "the Lord was with Joseph" (Gen. 39:3), everything that Joseph did prospered in his hand. In the different

> *He had every reason to complain, whine, grumble, scold, and lash out under the difficult circumstances in which he found himself. But he did not do any such thing.*

circumstances that he faced, he focused on the positive:

1. He kept his trust in God.
2. He remained an honest man.
3. He exercised patience.
4. He was diligent.
5. He was deferential.
6. He did not let the devil pervert his thoughts.
7. He focused on constructive habits.

Instead of using his time to blame and curse at others, Joseph blessed others. That is why, when his brothers came into Egypt during the famine to get food, he revealed himself to them and was able to say:

> "Please come near to me." So they came near. Then he said: "I am Joseph your brother, whom you sold into Egypt. But now, do not therefore be grieved or angry with yourselves because you sold me here; for God sent me before you to preserve life. For these two years the famine has been in the land, and there are still five years in which there will be neither plowing nor harvesting. And God sent me before you to preserve a posterity for you in the earth, and to save your lives by a great deliverance. So now it was not you who sent me here, but God; and He has made me a father to Pharaoh, and lord of all his house, and a ruler throughout all the land of Egypt." (Gen. 45:4–9, NKJV)

We can all learn about the power of positive living from Joseph. Although the devil threw everything at him to turn him into a bitter and miserable person, Joseph did not give in or give up. Instead of focusing on his negative situation, he lived with a consciousness of—

1. Providence—he recognized that God is sovereign in the darkest moments of life.
2. Forgiveness—he found ways of forgiving those who sought to hurt him.
3. Affirmation—he spoke to the positive qualities of those about him.

4. Connection—he connected positively with those who were with him, even in prison.
5. Kindness—he shared his knowledge and wisdom with those who were open to him.
6. Service—he was ready to serve where he was called.
7. Productivity—he did not waste time on things without value. Yes, like Joseph, a positive person, is open to the blessings of God. With eyes focused on God, the perfectly positive one will live in tranquility.

Take a Moment

Write down the blessing that the above reading has brought to your mind today and for which you would wish to thank the Lord.

_____
_____
_____
_____
_____
_____

Further, write down a special blessing that you would wish to ask the Lord to give you.

_____
_____
_____
_____
_____
_____

Then, write down how and with whom you would wish to share your blessing.

_____
_____
_____
_____
_____
_____

The Blessings of a Godly Character

The LORD was with Joseph, and he was a successful man; and he was in the house of his master the Egyptian. And his master saw that the LORD was with him and that the LORD made all he did to prosper in his hand. So Joseph found favor in his sight, and served him. Then he made him overseer of his house, and all that he had he put under his authority. So it was, from the time that he had made him overseer of his house and all that he had, that the LORD blessed the Egyptian's house for Joseph's sake; and the blessing of the LORD was on all that he had in the house and in the field. Thus he left all that he had in Joseph's hand, and he did not know what he had except for the bread which he ate. (Gen. 39:2–6, NKJV)

> If you want to enjoy God's favor, you must seek to develop a good character, for, as it is said, "Character is everything."

35.

The Blessings of a Godly Character

I am sure you have met them—people who have left you wondering what is deep inside their character. Their behavior has left you thinking that money means more to them than morals. When I have heard people commending the 45th president of the United States, acknowledging that he has a few flaws but that he is a good business man who can help the economy, I have to say that they are truly mixed up concerning the benefits of a good character.

My comment leads me back to the story of Joseph, who is considered in Scripture to be a person of stellar character. Here is a brief reflection on his life.

> The LORD was with Joseph, and he was a successful man, and he was in the house of his master the Egyptian. And his master saw that the LORD was with him and that the LORD made all he did to prosper in his hand. So Joseph found favor in his sight, and served him. Then he made him overseer of his house, and all that he had he put under his authority. (Gen. 39:2–4, NKJV)

One might say that Joseph's life could not always have been described in this way. His life started with a few flaws, for his father had indulged him by showing him preference above his brothers. He was, therefore, self-centered and exacting. However, after being sold into slavery, he began to grow in ways that led to the kind of characterization we read in Genesis 39. His character's better qualities began to shine in Potiphar's house and still more when he was in prison and when he was promoted to be the governor of Egypt. He was greatly admired by the king and everyone else.

Here is a list of fourteen most impressive qualities I have noted about Joseph's character and which I have argued should be emulated.

1. His confidence in God—it was obvious to anyone who came in contact with him.
2. His industriousness—even in prison, he found time to be useful. It is said, "The devil finds work for idle hands." (Or, "idle hands are the devil's workshop.") The devil could not use Joseph's hands.
3. His caring, compassionate, sympathetic attitude—Joseph's fellow prisoners felt these qualities.
4. His steadfastness—he kept his focus on his dream despite the false accusation that got him in prison.
5. His self-control—he never lost his cool even though he had reason to get angry.
6. His faithfulness—his master could trust him to be overseer of his house because he had shown that he was not a slave to evil.
7. His uprightness, integrity, and purity—he upheld what was right rather than what was wrong.
8. His decisiveness—in the moment of temptation, he did not have time to think for long. He did not dilly dally but quickly made up his mind to get away from evil.
9. His principles and values were founded on the utmost moral standard.
10. His wisdom and presence of mind were keen.
11. His patience—he was not easily frustrated. He had to wait for two years after the butler got out of prison before his case was brought before the king.
12. His humility—when he was brought before the king to interpret the king's dream, he gave credit to God for providing him wisdom.
13. His forgiveness of the butler and his brothers is exemplary. He did not retain any resentment or vengefulness.
14. His dignity—amid adversity and prosperity he maintained laudable self-respect. He would not condescend. He would not demean himself.

What are some blessings that flow from such character qualities?

1. Happiness. There are many words for "blessed" in the Bible, but the one that is used in the Beatitudes is the Greek word *makarios*, which means "to make happy." The blessed are happy.
2. Favor from God. The blessed are favored, or are the favorites, of God.
3. Well-being. The blessed have peace of mind and tranquility of soul (Matt. 5:9).

4. A good name. The blessed are respected. "A good name is more desirable than great riches" (Prov. 22:1, NIV).
5. Purity of heart. "Blessed are the pure in heart: for they shall see God" (Matt. 5:8, KJV).
6. Inheritance of the earth (Matt. 5:5). The blessed are at times not only advanced in this world but in the world to come.

He had to wait for two years after the butler got out of prison before his case was brought before the king.

Joseph got his blessings in Egypt, but he had more—a place in the Promised Land and a place in the kingdom of God. Character, it is said, is the only thing that we can take with us into the kingdom of God.

Take a Moment

Write down the blessing that the above reading has brought to your mind today and for which you would wish to thank the Lord.
_____
_____
_____
_____
_____
_____

Further, write down a special blessing that you would wish to ask the Lord to give you.
_____
_____
_____
_____
_____
_____

Then, write down how and with whom you would wish to share your blessing.
_____
_____
_____
_____
_____
_____

The Blessings of Truthfulness

So it was, from the time that he had made him overseer of his house and all that he had, that the LORD blessed the Egyptian's house for Joseph's sake; and the blessing of the LORD was on all that he had in the house and in the field. Thus he left all that he had in Joseph's hand, and he did not know what he had except for the bread which he ate. (Gen. 39:5, 6, NKJV).

> What a contrast between Joseph and Mrs. Potiphar! Joseph told the truth, while Mrs. Potiphar told a lie. In his book, *Soul of Fire*, novelist Terry Goodkind wrote, "That is the curse of lying, Sister. Once you place that crown of the liar upon your head, you can take it off again, but it leaves a stain for all time."

36.

The Blessings of Truthfulness

As the probe into the Russian interference into the 2016 elections drew to a conclusion, the attorneys and other advisors to the president were extremely fearful that the president would sit down to be questioned by Special Counsel Robert Muller and his team. The attorneys and advisors were worried that any sitting down would cause the president to perjure himself. A sad commentary, we need to say, for the leader of the world's most respected democracy to be so distrusted for not being able to speak the truth. As many know, one of the essential qualities of effective leadership is truth-telling.

This is one of the areas in which Joseph excelled in his service in Egypt. He was truthful in the house of Potiphar and faithful in his service before Pharaoh. Greatest of all, he was honest to his God. This is why I cannot stop reflecting on the text that captures the core of Joseph's life, namely:

> The LORD was with Joseph, and he was a successful man; and he was in the house of his master the Egyptian. And his master saw that the Lord was with him and that the LORD made all he did to prosper in his hand. So Joseph found favor in his sight, and served him. Then he made him overseer of his house, and all that he had he put under his authority. So it was, from the time that he had made him overseer of his house and all that he had, that the LORD blessed the Egyptian's house for Joseph's sake; and the blessing of the LORD was on all that he had in the house and in the field. Thus he left all that he had in Joseph's hand, and he did not know what he had except for the read which he ate. (Gen. 39:2–6, NKJV)

What a powerful quality to find in a leader! At a time when the world is confronting a dearth of truth, it is significant when one can find a leader who is willing to tell the truth no matter what. In fact, among the greatest reasons to tell the truth are the following:

1. Truth frees the heart. It keeps the soul at peace.

2. Truth demonstrates integrity of character. It comes from within, not from some external pressure.
3. Truth also builds a strengthened character.
4. Truth demonstrates that one is willing to take responsibility.
5. Truth creates credibility, trust, and respect.
6. Truth helps us to make effective decisions.
7. Truth helps people to confront reality.
8. Truth helps to build trusting relationships.
9. Truth serves as a wall of protection.
10. Truth is self-evident. When you tell it—even if it is at first ridiculed—it will ultimately come to the fore.

Let us not forget that the truth brings blessings not only to ourselves but also to the community in which we live. In the book of Proverbs, we are told: "He who speaks truth declares righteousness, but a false witness, deceit" (Prov. 12:17, NKJV). What marvelous blessings! Telling the truth, we have—

1. No fear of being found to being a liar.
2. No need to pack a lie on a lie.
3. No corruption of the mind.
4. No searing of the conscience.
5. No need to fear the wrath of the divine.

Joseph's life stood out because he was a truth-teller. He had a moral compass to his life. He spoke the truth and lived the truth. He was diligent in business, carrying out his duties as one serving the Lord. He was thorough in all he did. He was consistent in doing the little things. He was not a prevaricator. He was a truth-teller. He was loyal. He stood by those whom he served. No wonder Potiphar and the prison guard trusted him so profoundly and he was promoted as he was.

Such reflection on Joseph should make us ask:

1. How forthright are we in all that we do and speak?
2. How carefully do we do what we need to do?
3. How well do we keep our accounting books?
4. How faithful are we in the development of our character?

We need to ask these questions with seriousness, for we are not to forget that God rewards those who are truth-tellers. Joseph is truly an example.

Take a Moment

Write down the blessing that the above reading has brought to your mind today and for which you would wish to thank the Lord.

_____
_____
_____
_____
_____
_____

Further, write down a special blessing that you would wish to ask the Lord to give you.

_____
_____
_____
_____
_____
_____

Then, write down how and with whom you would wish to share your blessing.

_____
_____
_____
_____
_____
_____

The Blessings of Principled Living

For this you know, that no fornicator, unclean person, nor covetous man, who is an idolater, has any inheritance in the kingdom of Christ and God. (Eph. 5:5, NKJV)

> We bless the world when we take a moral stance. Morality is not just speaking the right words but taking the right stance.

37.

The Blessings of Principled Living

While driving on a highway, I turned on my car radio and was shocked to hear the rant of one individual, extolling the value of money over morality. He repeated in an aggressive voice, "So long as the United States president has made money for himself, and the economy is booming, we should not worry about his principles." The word, "What!!!" escaped my lips. I felt like changing the station and getting away from such "stupidity," but I tolerated it for a moment. Then I asked the question that was pressing on my mind, namely, "Does morality matter anymore?" My one question generated a flurry of other questions, just as if I were in one of my college ethics classrooms. Do we need to care about morality and principles when the economy is booming? Do we need to worry about what it means to "Love our neighbors," if we have money? Should we care about justice when we have money? Should we pay attention to questions of decency when we have money? Do we still need to pay attention to other citizens' lives in our community when we have money? Do we need to care about the preservation of the forests if we have money? Should we care about the poisoning of the water, so long as we have money? Does the appetite for the more comfortable life that money can buy push us out of the line of morality? Yes, numerous questions kept spinning in my head. I do not know that I can remember them all, except to say that they all ask about the connection between money and morality.

Human history is full of examples of how money trumps morality.

Remember Bernard L. Madoff? He died in prison because of the millions he stole from his clients through his Ponzi scheme. Remember Judas and how he sold Jesus for thirty pieces of silver? (Matt. 26:15). And remember how Joseph's brothers sold him for twenty shekels of silver? (Gen. 37:28). I mentioned Joseph last because, through divine providence, he became the governor of Egypt. And although he rose to such a high governmental position, Joseph refused to allow money or sexual immorality to corrupt him. He stands as a contrast to many within our contemporary legislative frame who seem to be selling their morality for money or sex and some other little favors that are upholding their image.

Yes, I like Joseph, for he was different from many around him who lived immorally through their money and positions of authority. When confronting a great temptation in Potiphar's house, Joseph made his decision to say, "So how could I do such a great evil and sin against God?" (Gen. 39:9, HCSB). He trusted God and did not compromise with money, sex, or anything else.

Joseph remembered well that God was to lead his life. His conscience was wide awake when he confronted temptation. Joseph did not allow the temptations to compromise his morals. When tempted, his resolve was, "I will not do that."

Yes, God is always ready to help us when we face situations of moral compromise. Through his strong moral values, Joseph speaks to us sweetly, yet sternly, "Don't do that." "Don't say that." "Don't go there." "Respect others." "Do not demean them because they do not have the resources that you have." And so on. Yes, those of us who want to live with high morality should listen when God speaks. We should not allow money to corrupt or compromise our morality.

Think about the following. Most of the people we admire in history are those who gave up wealth for serving others. Moses, Jesus, Francis of Assisi, Gautama Siddhartha, and Elijah Mohammed, Martin Luther King Jr., Mohandas Ghandi, Mother Teressa, etc., each counting service over wealth. I do not say that, if you give up your money, you are automatically going to be counted worthy before God, for there are those who deny themselves of life's resources as a way of gaining favors. What is of greatest concern to me is the moment we have come to in the world, when there is a loss concerning the blessings of morality and principles.

This is why I invited us to think about Joseph. By following a principled life:

1. He was favored in the eyes of God.
2. He was honorable before all those who related to him.
3. He suffered no regrets.
4. He did not need to rationalize his actions.
5. He reaped the reward of a disciplined life.
6. He enjoyed long-term happiness.
7. He never got distracted.
8. He was able to show who he was and who he was becoming.
9. He was able to enjoy the peace of God.

Take a Moment

Write down the blessing that the above reading has brought to your mind today and for which you would wish to thank the Lord.

_____
_____
_____
_____
_____

Further, write down a special blessing that you would wish to ask the Lord to give you.

_____
_____
_____
_____
_____

Then, write down how and with whom you would wish to share your blessing.

_____
_____
_____
_____
_____

The Blessings of Resiliency

Joseph called the name of the firstborn Manasseh: "For God has made me forget all my toil and all my father's house." And the name of the second he called Ephraim: "For God has caused me to be fruitful in the land of my affliction" (Gen. 41:51, 52, NKJV).

> In places we might least expect them, we can find our blessings, for God has hidden His blessings everywhere. It is only for us to find them.

38.

The Blessings of Resiliency

Many years ago, a group of us visited the Crystal Cathedral, which at the time was one of the jewels in Garden Grove, California. It was founded by Dr. Robert Schuller, who was principally known for the weekly Hour of Power television program, which he began hosting in 1970 until his retirement in 2010. At the end of our tour of the cathedral, Dr. Schuller gave us a brief presentation on his dream. He noted how God had taken him through hard times, yet, through providence and personal persistence, God guided him to the realization of his dream, as reflected in the cathedral. As he shared his dream, he used one of those memorable maxims, which he was so effective at sharing: "Tough times don't last, but tough people do." I have never forgotten the maxim. It has helped me through moments when I felt that I have been in a maze.

When I think of the maxim, it also causes me to reflect on Joseph's time in the pit, his being sold as a slave, and then his being lied upon by the wife of his master. Her lie allowed him to spend time in an Egyptian jail. All of the negative experiences could have gotten him down, but his spirit rose as he felt the leading of his father's God. I say "his father's God" because I am reflecting on the fact that his father Jacob must have shared the hardships of his life with him—especially the twenty years that he had spent in Padan Aram with his uncle Laban. Jacob must have told Joseph how his uncle tricked him concerning Rachel, the first woman he wanted to marry, and how his uncle sought to steal his wages. In Genesis 31, we read part of Jacob's complaint to his two wives about wanting to leave Laban's house and return to his father's house in Canaan: "Yet your father has not been fair with me. He has changed my pay ten times. But God did not let him hurt me" (Gen. 31:7). After Jacob left Laban's house and Laban went after him, Jacob's anger boiled over, as the story recounts.

> Then Jacob became angry and argued with Laban. Jacob said to Laban, "What have I done wrong? What is my sin that made you run after me? What things of your house have you found by looking through all that belongs to me? Set it here in front of my brothers and your brothers, so they may judge between us. During these twenty years I have been with you, your female goats and sheep have not lost a young one. And I have not eaten the sheep of your flocks. I did not bring to you those that were torn by wild animals. I took the loss upon myself. You had me pay for what was carried away during the day or during the night. This is the way it was for me. I suffered from heat during the day, and from cold during the night. And I could not sleep. I have been in your house twenty years. I worked for you fourteen years for your two daughters, and six years for your flock. And you changed my pay ten times. If the God of my father, the God of Abraham and the fear of Isaac, had not been with me, for sure you would have sent me away with nothing. God has seen my suffering and the work of my hands. So He spoke sharp words to you last night." (Gen. 31:36–42, NLT)

Joseph must have been familiar with his father's story, but, in leaving home, he came to know God for himself. In the moments he felt truly challenged, he was resilient. He named his first son, Manasseh, meaning,

"God has made me forget completely my hardship and my parental home." He named his second Ephraim, meaning "fruitful," because, he said, "God has made me fertile in the land of my affliction" (Gen. 41:51, 52, from https://www.rabbilewin.net/parashat-vayechi-our-childrens-jewish-connection). The reality is that Joseph did not spend time "whining" and "complaining," rather, he devoted his life to constant praise to God. Despite the downward course of his life, Joseph was able to bounce back. When he was taken out of jail to serve as governor, he did not spend time reciting and analyzing all of the bad things that had happened to him. When he met his brothers, who had come to Egypt to buy food, he made it clear to them that he had forgiven them, and that what they meant for evil God had turned into a blessing.

As the new generations of Israelites came along, they heard of Joseph's legacy. They heard of his request to have his bones to be taken back to the Promised Land. They heard that he did not allow the difficulties of his life to define him. He did not let his failures label him. He never worried about his past. He focused on his future and built up such a healthy identity that Pharaoh was forced to take notice of him.

I do not know what difficulties you are confronting. I do not know what challenges you might be experiencing. What I do know is that the God who made Joseph as resilient as he was, has the same resources to give you. All you need to do is cooperate with God so that He can bestow blessings on you as he made them available to Joseph.

Take a Moment

Write down the blessing that the above reading has brought to your mind today and for which you would wish to thank the Lord.

_____
_____
_____
_____
_____
_____

Further, write down a special blessing that you would wish to ask the Lord to give you.

_____
_____
_____
_____
_____
_____

Then, write down how and with whom you would wish to share your blessing.

_____
_____
_____
_____
_____
_____

The Blessings of Forgiveness

And Joseph said to his brothers, "Please come near to me." So they came near. Then he said: "I am Joseph your brother, whom you sold into Egypt. But now, do not therefore be grieved or angry with yourselves because you sold me here; for God sent me before you to preserve life. For these two years the famine has been in the land, and there are still five years in which there will be neither plowing nor harvesting. And God sent me before you to preserve a posterity for you in the earth, and to save your lives by a great deliverance. So now it was not you who sent me here, but God; and He has made me a father to Pharaoh, and lord of all his house, and a ruler throughout all the land of Egypt." (Gen. 45:4–8, NKJV)

> One of the greatest blessings of life is forgiveness. God forgives us. We forgive ourselves. We forgive others. That is how the circle and cycle of forgiveness grows.

39.

The Blessings of Forgiveness

At a time when we are facing angry protests and riots across the United States and in many cities of the world in reaction to the killing of George Floyd and other black men and women, at the hands of some cold-hearted police personnel, I have heard many people asking, "How can we forgive such brutality?" Inasmuch as I do not agree with any broad-based negative view of the police, I cannot pretend that the question has never entered my mind, for I have also suffered from what is called "systemic racism." However, when I think of characters like Joseph and Jesus, I have to ask, "Who am I that I should not forgive?" Among the last words that Jesus spoke from the cross were, "Father, forgive them, for they do not know what they are doing" (Luke 23:34, NIV). Jesus is the great forgiver, but each of us has to learn like Joseph what it means to forgive. Just imagine the following.

1. What must it have been for Joseph to grow up around older brothers that resented him! In some ways, he could have blamed himself for sharing his dreams with his brothers, who thought him arrogant for suggesting that they were someday going to bow down to him.
2. When his father sent him to visit the brothers who were tending sheep in Dothan, his father did not know how deeply his brother's resented him. Their resentment boiled up so much that they thought of murdering him.
3. But at the intervention of one brother, they stripped him and put him into a pit.
4. Then when they saw some slave traders passing by, they took him out of the pit and sold him to them for twenty pieces of silver.
5. On reaching Egypt, the traders sold him to Potiphar, one of Pharaoh's army chiefs.
6. Joseph served faithfully in Potiphar's house, until he was promoted to be head steward.

7. But soon, Mrs. Potiphar set her eyes on him with sexual interest. And when he would not yield to her advances, she tried to rape him, and when she failed, she told a big lie on him to her husband. We do not know whether Potiphar believed her lie, but, to please her, he threw Joseph into jail.
8. Joseph would spend the next ten years in jail, but the God he served was watching and allowed him to come out of those circumstances and become second in command to the king of Egypt.
9. The great famine that broke out in all of the middle eastern regions would lead the brothers of Joseph to visit Egypt to buy food from the stock that Joseph had wisely secured through the seven years of plenty.
10. On seeing the brothers, Joseph recognized them but did not reveal to them who he was until their third trip to Egypt for food.
11. After revealing himself to his brothers, he also made it known that he had forgiven their treacherous acts when he said—

"Come close to me." Then he said, "I am your brother Joseph, the one you sold into Egypt! And now, do not be distressed and do not be angry with yourselves for selling me here, because it was to save lives that God sent me ahead of you. For two years now there has been famine in the land, and for the next five years there will be no plowing and reaping. But God sent me ahead of you to preserve for you a remnant on earth and to save your lives by a great deliverance. So then, it was not you who sent me here, but God. He made me a father to Pharaoh, Lord of his entire household and ruler of all Egypt" (Gen. 45:4–7, NIV).

What a great opportunity! Joseph could have taken revenge on his brothers, but he did not. He was, at this point, exalted to the highest position of power such that he could have had them ordered to be killed, or he could have imprisoned them for the rest of their lives. He could have sent them away empty. He could have pretended not to know them. But he did not do what the natural propensities of a human heart seek to do. Instead of taking vengeance, he forgave his brothers.

Joseph rid his heart of any anger and resentment toward his brothers. Max Lucado says that, in Joseph, "bitterness never staked its claim. Anger never metastasized into hatred. His heart never hardened; his resolve never vanished. He not only survived; he thrived" (*You Will Get Through It*, p. 7). In effect, Joseph did not hold onto his past. He turned to his present and the future. If given the chance, he could say with the apostle

Paul, "And we know that all things work together for good to those who love God, to those who are the called according to His purpose" (Rom. 8:28, NKJV).

Joseph's forgiving attitude towards his brothers and their subsequent relationship with him is a powerful model for us today. I now ask those who are holding onto their anger, resentment, hurt, and grudges if they have considered the blessings that they might receive if they were willing to forgive. Over the years, I have thought of or collected some 25 forgiveness blessings that I list here for your contemplation. The list is comprehensive but not exhaustive.

> *Joseph's forgiving attitude towards his brothers and their subsequent relationship with him is a powerful model for us today.*

1. Forgiveness means that we have been privileged to hear the sweet words, "You are forgiven."
2. We have been given grace—the compassion of God.
3. We have been given redemption in Christ.
4. We have been given unadulterated joy in Christ.
5. We can now receive the merits of Christ.
6. Forgiveness transforms relationships.
7. It gives us access to the presence of God.
8. It brings peace in the heart.
9. It brings health into the body.
10. Forgiveness removes jealousies and resentment.
11. Violence disappears in the presence of forgiveness.
12. It destroys suspicion.
13. It opens the way to a positive future.
14. Forgiveness cleans the conscience of guilt and shame.
15. It frees us to love God, ourselves, and others.
16. It helps us to grow spiritually.
17. Forgiveness allows us to be more open to the nature of our sin.
18. It allows for answered prayers.
19. It helps us to testify to the power of God.
20. The principle found all through the Bible is that forgiveness is God's gift.
21. By forgiving, we will be able to live a life of complete joy and freedom.
22. By forgiving our families, friends and foes can live together.

23. By forgiving, we can live next to each other without any hard feelings.
24. By forgiving, we can smile and shake hands without thinking that someone might put a dagger in our sides.
25. Forgiveness creates many differences in our lives.

Whenever I hear people preaching hate and claiming that they cannot forgive, I fear for them, for I know that, without forgiveness, they will ever live in their brokenness. Dr. Martin Luther King, Jr., stated in a sermon on Sunday, August 12, 1962: "We must develop and maintain the capacity to forgive," for "he who is devoid of the power to forgive is devoid of the power to love.... There is some good in the worst of us and some evil in the best of us. When we discover this, we are less liable to hate our enemies" (Martin Luther King, Jr., sermon, Ebenezer Baptist Church, quoted in *Boston Record American*, Sept. 12, 1962, p. 25; *Las Vegas Review-Journal*, April 14, 1968, p. 56). So, while forgiveness might be hard, we must understand that our world will never last without it.

Have you ever imagined a world without forgiveness? What a sad world it would be! It would be a world of total curses, a world with no hope, no love, no peace, no happiness, no healing, no song of delight, no marital survival, no second or third or fourth chances, and no possibility of reconciled relationships. Lack of forgiveness means death. Forgiveness is God's greatest gift to us.

Take a Moment

Write down the blessing that the above reading has brought to your mind today and for which you would wish to thank the Lord.

_____
_____
_____
_____
_____
_____

Further, write down a special blessing that you would wish to ask the Lord to give you.

_____
_____
_____
_____
_____
_____

Then, write down how and with whom you would wish to share your blessing.

_____
_____
_____
_____
_____
_____

The Blessings of Discernment

And Pharaoh said to his servants, "Can we find such a one as this, a man in whom is the Spirit of God?" Then Pharaoh said to Joseph, "Inasmuch as God has shown you all this, there is no one as discerning and wise as you." (Gen. 41:38, 39, NKJV)

> Although God's wisdom is available to everyone, it only goes to those who are truly connected with God. Those who have a need for wisdom must actively seek it, for God has promised to give it.

40.

The Blessings of Discernment

In our age, when there is a shortage of leaders with discernment, we need to find people with character like Joseph, whose wisdom guided Egypt during one of its gravest times of crisis. As we think of the crisis of the Covid 19 pandemic, we need more leaders like Joseph. When Pharaoh needed a man to stabilize the economy of Egypt, he found Joseph. As Scripture portrays, Joseph was a man with practical wisdom. He had the uncanny ability to look deep into things, insomuch that he was able to avoid present and future disasters.

When we are first introduced to the young Joseph in Canaan, he is presented as a dreamer (Gen. 37:1–10) who had the gift of interpreting dreams (Gen. 40, 41). Of course, he did not really seem wise when he shared his dreams with his brothers. The sharing of those dreams led to the jealousy that encouraged his brothers to sell him into Egyptian slavery (Gen. 37:18–36). However, he grew in his wisdom—to the extent that he was able to interpret the baker's and the butler's dreams. And later, he was called to interpret Pharaoh's dreams. None of the Egyptian wise men were able to interpret the dreams, but Joseph was. His interpretation of Pharaoh's dream led Pharaoh to appoint him to be second in command in the administration of Egypt.

The wisdom of the Egyptians worked in the magical arts, but it was paralyzed before the wisdom of the divine. When Pharaoh asked that a man be found in whom "the spirit of the Lord is" (Gen. 41:38), he might not have understood what he meant in depth, but, when Joseph interpreted his dreams, he sensed that God was with Joseph, even as Potiphar noted before (Gen. 40:2). A truth spoken of in multiple places in the Bible is that God was with them. Daniel got the same commendation (see Dan. 5:12, 14; 6:3). Like Joseph, Daniel declared that the source of wisdom was with God. We read in Proverbs, "The fear of the Lord is the beginning of wisdom" (Prov. 9:10, NKJV). The apostle James confirms, "If any of you lack wisdom, you should ask God" (James 1:5, NIV).

> *The wisdom of the Egyptians worked in the magical arts, but it was paralyzed before the wisdom of the divine.*

Yes, Joseph's most critical display of divine wisdom became evident as he managed the food crisis in Egypt (Gen. 41:46–57; 47:13–26). Wherever he was—whether it was in Potiphar's house, in prison, or before Pharaoh—he depended on God. His wisdom and discernment enabled him to save his extended family. Here is an outline of how effective his wisdom worked.

1. It allowed him to discern the crisis that was about to take place in Egypt and to know what to do about it.
2. It allowed him to hone his skills for effective management, beginning with his plan of action in building the grain silos.
3. He was able to communicate clearly with Pharaoh and all other parties on what to do in all the eventualities of the crisis.
4. He developed good policies so that there could be extensive cooperation for the land use and produce retention.
5. He was effective as a negotiator with the people so that more and more land and food supplies could be stored.
6. He set up a system of food distribution that included people beyond Egypt.
7. He was able to make the right kinds of decisions for the administration of the kingdom.

There is no question that Joseph was wise and discerning. He was not a prisoner to self-trust. This is why he was able to distinguish between right and wrong. He constantly sought the guidance of God and was able to bring to the Egyptians, his family, and future generations the wonderful blessings that he did.

Discernment is truly one of the most important blessings that God has given to humanity. As we face the present darkness of our world, we need to pray: "Lord, please, give us discernment." The apostles say we need discernment to distinguish between true and the false spirits (1 Cor. 12:10; 2 Peter 1:3). We need to train ourselves to do so (Heb. 5:14) because, as the apostle John says, "Many deceivers have gone out into the world" (2 John 1:7, ESV). Solomon prayed, and the Lord gave him the gift of discernment and other gifts as well (1 Kings 3).

Take a Moment

Write down the blessing that the above reading has brought to your mind today and for which you would wish to thank the Lord.
_____
_____
_____
_____
_____
_____

Further, write down a special blessing that you would wish to ask the Lord to give you.
_____
_____
_____
_____
_____
_____

Then, write down how and with whom you would wish to share your blessing.
_____
_____
_____
_____
_____
_____

The Blessings on Joseph

The Lord was with Joseph, and he was a successful man; and he was in the house of his master the Egyptian. And his master saw that the LORD was with him ... the Lord blessed the Egyptian's house for Joseph's sake; and the blessing of the LORD was on all that he had ... (Gen. 39:2, 3, 5)

> It is a blessing to live with the consciousness that God is present with us to protect, provide, pilot, and strengthen and to give us success in every endeavor. "If God is for us, who can be against us?"

41.

The Blessings on Joseph

I am writing this reflection on the morning after a national election in the United States of America, where there were many winners and losers. I am wondering how many who have won or lost are giving God praise for their victories or their losses. How many of us understand that God rules in the affairs of nations, governments, and kingdoms, and in people's lives? And regardless of the outcome, we should consider the wins and the losses the Lord's blessing.

I really enjoy reading the following passage: "And the LORD was with Joseph, and he became a successful man, serving in the household of his Egyptian master" (Gen. 39:2, HCSB). Joseph might have considered his situation a setback or an accursed time, but he was faithful to God in all the days of hardship, and God led him out of his distress. He lived his life without recrimination and in such a way that it could be said of him, "The LORD was with him" (Gen. 39:3, KJV). The history of his life and his successes as a slave in Potiphar's house while in prison and throughout the time that he administered the governorship of Egypt are phenomenal.

Not for a moment did Joseph forget who led in his life and had elevated him to the highest leadership position. After his successful administration in taking Egypt through one of its severest famines, Joseph never ran around saying like Nebuchadnezzar, " 'Look at this great city of Babylon! By my own mighty power, I have built this beautiful city as my royal residence to display my majestic splendor.' " (Dan. 4:30, NLT). No, Joseph remembered that God rules in the affairs of humanity (see Dan. 4:17). Nebuchadnezzar, on the other hand, forgot that it was God who had set him on high. At one point God called him "my servant" (Jer. 43:10). But he had to be reminded, while being the most powerful leader on earth at the time, that he was still under obligation to God. He became confused, for a while, at least, forgetting that, at one time in his life, he had declared the Lord the supreme ruler of all (see Dan. 2). Then he became prosperous and then pompous. Therefore, God brought him down to a point of humiliation by sending him off to eat grass for seven years. Through that experience, he learned a lesson of humility, and, when he lifted up his eyes to God, he was re-established on his throne. Read the details of the story in Daniel 4.

My point is simply that "God can exalt," and "God can take down." Even if it may be true that not everyone who ever came into office did so fairly, yet the hand of God is within the frame. Despite foolish declarations, it needs to be understood that God is superintending and will step in to rule the tide of evil. He will show up to make known his power. This might call for patient waiting, and such is what Joseph understood and never lost sight of.

When there is so much talk of corruption and the like, we must declare that we need a few Josephs in the land. If you are reading this reflection, I ask you to pray that God will help raise up people like Joseph.

Let me remind you, dear reader, that you do not need to be in a high position of leadership to live a life like Joseph. When Joseph was serving in the house of his Egyptian master, it was said of him: "The Lord was with Joseph." Sometimes the blessings that God is bringing in a life are not seen immediately. Sometimes people are left to struggle like Joseph before the blessings shine forth. After God showed Joseph through his dream that he was to be a leader in his family and community, many negative things happened in his life. Betrayed by his brothers, Joseph found himself in a pit. He was sold as a slave in Potiphar's house and was finally thrown into prison. It would not be until about thirteen years later that he would see God's promise fulfilled when he became the governor of Egypt. Yet, he was steadfast in his love and service to God.

Let us live our lives for the blessings that God's presence brings. By His presence:

1. We are privileged with the manifestation of glory.
2. We can know we are under the splendor of love.
3. We have a sense of eternal security.
4. We have a sense of comfort and peace.
5. We are strengthened to face life with courage and joy.
6. We are guided in the way of righteousness.
7. We have confidence that we are protected.
8. We live in the light instead of in the darkness.
9. We have the companionship of the divine.
10. We are favored with revelation.

Without God's presence, we will never be truly connected to the eternal source of blessings. We will be left in the midst of darkness and in the pit of despair.

Take a Moment

Write down the blessing that the above reading has brought to your mind today and for which you would wish to thank the Lord.

_____
_____
_____
_____
_____
_____

Further, write down a special blessing that you would wish to ask the Lord to give you.

_____
_____
_____
_____
_____
_____

Then, write down how and with whom you would wish to share your blessing.

_____
_____
_____
_____
_____
_____

Blessed to Bless Others

When Joseph's brothers saw that their father was dead, they said, "Perhaps Joseph will hate us, and may actually repay us for all the evil which we did to him." So they sent messengers to Joseph, saying, "Before your father died he commanded, saying, 'Thus you shall say to Joseph: "I beg you, please forgive the trespass of your brothers and their sin; for they did evil to you." ' Now, please, forgive the trespass of the servants of the God of your father." And Joseph wept when they spoke to him. Then his brothers also went and fell down before his face, and they said, "Behold, we are your servants." Joseph said to them, "Do not be afraid, for am I in the place of God? But as for you, you meant evil against me; but God meant it for good, in order to bring it about as it is this day, to save many people alive. Now therefore, do not be afraid; I will provide for you and your little ones." And he comforted them and spoke kindly to them. (Gen. 50:15–21, NKJV)

> It is of interest that we have to set aside this chapter to remember the importance of kindness and to make an extra effort to treat others (and ourselves) with gentleness and understanding. How many of us miss divine blessings by failing to use each day to pass on our blessings to others.

42.

Blessed to Bless Others

As a caravan from several Central American countries approached and camped at the southern border of the United States, seeking refuge from poverty and oppression, the president of the United States announced some of the harshest measures to block their entry. While the president tried to defend his policies, I began to ask what it means when people use the phrase, "God bless America." Does it not mean that the president and all who live in the United States really need to understand that, when God blesses a nation or a person, we are under obligation to bless others?

The latter is the great lesson that comes to us from the story of Joseph, who was sold as a slave in Egypt. He rose to prominence through the providence of God, becoming Pharaoh's chief administrator during a famine that would overtake Egypt (Gen. 41:46–57; 47:13–26). Pharaoh came to regard him highly. In fact, when he sent for his family to join him and the group of seventy individuals, including Joseph's father and brothers, joined Joseph in Egypt, Pharaoh personally welcomed them. Then he gave them the best land. They lived, multiplied, and became respectable citizens in Egypt for more than 400 years. But a time came when Egypt was unfriendly to them. The Bible tells the story:

> Now there arose a new king over Egypt, who did not know Joseph. And he said to his people, "Look, the people of the children of Israel are more and mightier than we; come, let us deal shrewdly with them, lest they multiply, and it happen, in the event of war, that they also join our enemies and fight against us, and so go up out of the land." Therefore they set taskmasters over them to afflict them with their burdens. And they built for Pharaoh supply cities, Pithom and Raamses. But the more they afflicted them, the more they multiplied and grew. And they were in dread of the children of Israel. So the Egyptians made the children of Israel serve with rigor. And they made their lives bitter with hard bondage—in mortar, in brick, and in all manner of service in the field. All their service in which they made them serve was with rigor. (Exod. 1:8–14, NKJV)

The second part of the story tells how the new Pharaoh brought jealousy, hatred and increasing pressure on the people of Israel. Conditions became so severe that, after the ten plagues that ravaged Egypt, the people escaped from Egypt under Moses' leadership. Wherever they passed through the territories of other nations, such as the Midianites and Moabites, they brought much fear. These nations were so fearful that they joined together to overcome Israel. Yet, they failed. So they hired Balaam to curse Israel (Num. 22). The curse did not work either. However, the nations found other ways to curse Israel. Not every Midianite or Moabite was part of the efforts to curse Israel. Some of the Midianites and Moabites joined up with Israel. Thus, we have the story of the Kenites (a Midianite family) who joined with the tribe of Levi and, later, Ruth the Moabitess, who, through marriage, became a part of the tribe of Judah. As a whole, however, the Midianites and Moabites who sought to hurt Israel were punished for their bad attitude toward Israel. Later, God delivered His divine pronouncement through the prophetic word in Psalms: "Moab is my washbasin" (Ps. 60:8, NIV). This was a harsh word of judgment against a nation that failed in its responsibility to be a blessing.

The point being emphasized is that, as people and nations, we are blessed so we can bless others. God is watching over the earth and is taking note of how we are passing the blessings that He has given us. The opportunities that we are provided to share our blessings are myriad. Here are at least twelve suggestions of what we can do. We can—

1. Speak a word of blessing into the lives of others.
2. Share a blessing with a kind gesture with whom we come in contact.
3. Encourage a fearful heart.
4. Comfort a grieving soul.
5. Care for someone in need.
6. Forgive those who trespass against us.
7. Support those who are around us.
8. Testify about what God has done in our lives.
9. Speak up for those who cannot speak for themselves.
10. Affirm those with whom we come in contact.
11. Act with integrity.
12. Volunteer in our community.

If you are having any difficulty passing on your blessings, ask yourself, why have you been so blessed? God blesses us to bless.

Take a Moment

Write down the blessing that the above reading has brought to your mind today and for which you would wish to thank the Lord.

_____
_____
_____
_____
_____

Further, write down a special blessing that you would wish to ask the Lord to give you.

_____
_____
_____
_____
_____

Then, write down how and with whom you would wish to share your blessing.

_____
_____
_____
_____
_____

Blessings from a Deathbed

And Joseph said to his brethren, "I am dying; but God will surely visit you, and bring you out of this land to the land of which He swore to Abraham, Isaac, and Jacob." Then Joseph took an oath from the children of Israel, saying, "God will surely visit you, and you shall carry up my bones from here." So Joseph died, being one hundred and ten years old; and they embalmed him, and he was put in a coffin in Egypt. (Gen. 50:24–26, NKJV)

> A deathbed is a rather challenging place to be, and yet it gives us one of life's most exceptional opportunities to pass on blessings to others. Just think today, if you are reading this chapter, what blessing you would wish to pass on to your children, other nearest of kin, friends, other near acquaintances, and the world at large.

43.

Blessings from a Deathbed

For quite a few years before he died and a few months before he completed his 105th year, our father talked often about his death wish. He would want to have all of his children about his bedside to pronounce a blessing on each one as he saw them. He said that, at its conclusion, he would like to pull up his feet into his bed, like Jacob, and die (see Gen. 47). Our father did not get to do as he wished, however, because, about five weeks before his death, he suffered a stroke that left him speechless. And, even though all his children visited his bedside, he could only squeeze our hands or hug us, and, at the last only blink his eyes, for he was reduced to silence.

Although Dad was not able to speak, those of us who traveled in to see him were gratified when we sang and prayed and recalled the history of his life and ours. Everyone who went to the bedside—children, doctors, nurses, and others—said they walked away with the assurance that they had received an exceptional blessing. Our assurance was strong because Dad was a man of faith, hope, love, and compassion, and, even in his silence, one sensed where his spirit was. We knew Dad was conscious most of the weeks he was lying on that deathbed. From the life he had lived, we knew that he was thinking about the subject on which he had preached so often. He framed the subject in many ways but most unforgettably as "Pageantry in the Sky." If you are wondering, the sermon was on the second coming of Christ, the hope of the people of God, the home of the saved, the redemption of the righteous, the resurrection, and whatever he could fit into the frame.

Yes, we did not hear final words from Dad, and some of us did not see his last smile or see him give up his last breath, but, with his having such a long life, we were able to take comfort in his passing and reflect on the influential life he had lived. Yes, standing there beside him caused us to look at the vulnerabilities of life and contemplate our own deathbed wishes.

I have talked about my dad, but I wonder how it must have been for the brothers of Joseph, as they stood about his deathbed. From the text in Genesis 50, we see how Joseph was making every effort to assure them that all would be well. The text of interest states:

> And Joseph said to his brethren, "I am dying; but God will surely visit you, and bring you out of this land to the land of which He swore to Abraham, to Isaac, and to Jacob." Then Joseph took an oath from the children of Israel, saying, "God will surely visit you, and you shall carry up my bones from here." So Joseph died, being one hundred and ten years old; and they embalmed him, and he was put in a coffin in Egypt. (Gen. 50:24–26, NKJV)

It was a critical moment for the brothers. They wanted to know whether Joseph had truly forgiven them. Was he still maintaining any resentment toward them, that his sons, Manasseh and Ephraim, might use as a pretext to revenge them? What was going to happen to them with reference to the Pharaoh? If such might have been their concerns, Joseph had powerful insights to give them. He wanted to share his blessings with them. He wanted to assure them that he had fixed things in a way that they would be alright. There was no need to do a deathbed reconciliation, as some individuals have had to do with a brother or a sister. All of that had been taken care of and would someday come to fruition when their children would be taken out of Egypt to go back home. The more significant issue now was to assure them that God's promise to Abraham of returning to the land of promise would be fulfilled.

When a child of God is passing from this life with the assurance that the loved ones that they leave behind will be taken care of, that is a real blessing. The Scriptures state that the dead know nothing.

> For the living know that they will die; but the dead know nothing, and they have no more reward, for the memory of them is forgotten. Also their love, their hatred, and their envy have now perished; nevermore will they have a share in anything done under the sun. (Eccles. 9:5, 6, NKJV)

We need to take care of all we can while we live. Let us bless those we can bless. Let us not wait until our deathbeds to share our dreams and blessings because we may not all have the opportunity like Isaac (Gen. 27:7) or Jacob (Gen. 47:29) or Joseph (Gen. 50:24) or like my Dad to pass on the final blessing. Every opportunity we have we need to take time to bless whoever we can bless. Speak a blessing into their lives.

Take a Moment

Write down the blessing that the above reading has brought to your mind today and for which you would wish to thank the Lord.

_____
_____
_____
_____
_____

Further, write down a special blessing that you would wish to ask the Lord to give you.

_____
_____
_____
_____
_____

Then, write down how and with whom you would wish to share your blessing.

_____
_____
_____
_____
_____

Finding a Blessed Place of Rest

Then Joseph took an oath from the children of Israel, saying, "God will surely visit you, and you shall carry up my bones from here." So Joseph died, being one hundred and ten years old, and they embalmed him, and he was put in a coffin in Egypt. (Gen. 50:25, 26, NKJV)

> A burial place can be blessed, not because of the committal prayer that is made by a minister but because the eye of God is overshadowing the place. God marks each grave to await the resurrection. Thus, while only a few have control over where they are buried, everyone can control their final destiny. Those who are faithful to God have a place of rest awaiting them in heaven.

44.

Finding a Blessed Place of Rest

How does it feel to be called an alien, a foreigner, or even identified as a criminal because you were not born in a particular country? How does it feel, even if you were born in a place, to be treated like a second or third-class citizen? Maybe you are someone who has attained to some position of prominence and have forgotten who you were and what it is like to be treated as a slave. Joseph didn't. When he became governor of Egypt, he never forgot what it felt like to have been sold as a slave, accused of rape, and put in an Egyptian prison. He was also premonished what his people might face after his death in the years of their sojourn in Egypt.

Through the providence of God, Joseph was rapidly promoted to the second in command of Egypt, next to Pharaoh. However, as one insightful commentator states, his rise was reason enough for him to be eyed negatively by some of the Egyptians. To them, he was an outsider and a criminal who had been sentenced to prison for the rape of the wife of a senior Egyptian official. When Joseph's brothers made their second trip to Egypt to buy food, and Joseph invited them to dine, their tables were separated. When it was discovered that Joseph was himself a Hebrew, he was scorned, for the Egyptians could not eat with the Hebrews because the Hebrews were shepherds.

When Joseph reached his time to die, he called his family around him and told them of his last wish. He asked that his bones be taken out of Egypt to Canaan.

Some might say how strange the request was, but it is not so uncommon. There are people from some of the countries in Africa and the African diaspora who want to be buried back home. The biblical text says:

> And Joseph said to his brethren, "I am dying; but God will surely visit you, and bring you out of this land to the land of which He swore to Abraham, to Isaac, and to Jacob." Then Joseph took an oath from the children of Israel, saying, "God will surely visit you, and you shall carry up my bones from here." So Joseph died, being one hundred and ten years old; and they embalmed him, and he was put in a coffin in Egypt. (Gen. 50:24–26, NKJV)

It was always in Joseph's mind that, although he was in a high position in Egypt, he had been a slave and his people would be slaves and would never be free while living in Egypt. Egypt always represented an alien territory to the Israelites. So, Joseph looked forward to the day when they would go back home. Therefore, he reminded them that they should carry his bones to the land of promise when they returned to Canaan. By taking his bones, they were to do as the Apostle Paul encouraged the Philippian church members to do—to forget the things that are to be left behind and to reach for the things that were before them, pressing toward the prize of the high calling of God in Christ Jesus (Phil. 3:13, 14). Joseph's family members were to look beyond Egypt's graves and beyond their sojourn in Egypt to the Promised Land, where they would be home and free.

Let me frame this in the perspective of the Christian resurrection by stating that our graves in this world are not what God intends for our last state to be. Beyond the grave, we are promised the resurrection life. However that will be, it is clear that the grave is not to be the resting place of the saved. Whether God will use our bones or our ashes to bring us back to life, I do not know, but like Joseph and the faithful of the ages, I know that God has in store for us a better life and a better country. The New Testament recalls the faith of the patriarchs and matriarchs of Hebrews 11, the apostles, martyrs, and everyone else who have their hope in Christ that one of these days Christ will come back to call His faithful ones from the grave (1 Thess. 4:16, 17; 1 Cor. 15; Rev. 20ff).

Yes, there is a powerful message in Joseph's last wish to take his bones back to the Promised Land. Hebrews states: "By faith Joseph, when he was dying, made mention of the departure of the children of Israel, and gave instructions concerning his bones" (Heb. 11:22, NKJV).

If someone were to ask you for your last wish—your deathbed wish—or to express your final dream, what would it be?

Take a Moment

Write down the blessing that the above reading has brought to your mind today and for which you would wish to thank the Lord.

_____
_____
_____
_____
_____
_____

Further, write down a special blessing that you would wish to ask the Lord to give you.

_____
_____
_____
_____
_____
_____

Then, write down how and with whom you would wish to share your blessing.

_____
_____
_____
_____
_____
_____

The Blessings We Leave Behind

Then Abraham breathed his last and died in a good old age, an old man and full of years, and was gathered to his people. (Gen. 25:8, NKJV)

So Isaac breathed his last and died, and was gathered to his people, being old and full of days. And his sons Esau and Jacob buried him. (Gen. 35:29, NKJV)

And when Jacob had finished commanding his sons, he drew his feet up into the bed and breathed his last, and was gathered to his people. (Gen. 49:33, NKJV)

So Joseph died, being one hundred and ten years old; and they embalmed him, and he was put in a coffin in Egypt. (Gen. 50:26, NKJV)

> In his play on Julius Caesar, William Shakespeare declares, "The evil that men do lives after them; the good is oft interred with their bones." But the prophet Malachi says, "A book of remembrance was written before him of those who feared the LORD and esteemed his name."

45.

The Blessings We Leave Behind

I have heard people say simplistically, "If you live long enough, death will take you out of this world." I have also heard someone say, "We have to live until we die." It is not very inspiring, but death is life's greatest inevitable. When we read that Abraham, Isaac, Jacob, Rachel, Joseph, and even Jesus and others "breathed" their last breath, we know that death is not about to escape any of us. It is the constant harbinger of our lives (see Gen. 25:8; 35:29; 49:33; 50:26; Mark 15:37). That is how it has been from the moment of the Fall, when death was pronounced on all humanity (see Gen. 2:17; 3:24; Rom. 5:12).

We read, in the words of Job, one of the greatest sages that ever lived:

> Man, who is born of woman
> Is of few days and full of trouble.
> He comes forth like a flower and fades away;
> He flees like a shadow and does not continue....
> So man lies down and does not rise.
> Till the heavens are no more,
> They will not awake
> Nor be roused from their sleep. (Job 14:1, 2, 12, NKJV)

Such reflection leaves us no doubt about the assurance that death will take us away from this world, some quietly, and some tragically. But a question remains about the legacy of blessings or the influence of the life that was lived and, more notably, of the sweet fragrance that each of us will leave behind.

While I was thinking of the many lives that have been senselessly snuffed out, I began to think about my father, who passed away. As I am writing this, this event is one year to the day, so I think of him passing at the ripe old age of just one month and a few days short of his 105th birthday. Throughout his life, he made it his practice to remind us of when

Jacob "breathed" his last. Dad wanted to do like Jacob, and he would quote the text:

> And when Jacob had finished commanding his sons, he drew his feet up into the bed and breathed his last, and was gathered to his people. (Gen. 49:33, NKJV)

In the latter part of his life, Dad would say the words above so often that it was almost intimidating. We wanted to know what he would have said if we were to stand at his bedside just as he breathed his last breath. Some of us were not present at his bedside to the end, but Dad had said enough in his life to know his thoughts of us. We did not always like all his witty comments, but he was profoundly wise and gracious with his evaluations. From the burial instructions he left and the many little notes of encouragement that we found in his study after his death, we can say that Dad left us a great legacy of blessings. And the blessings are so significant that we feel like the children of Abraham, Isaac, and Jacob with the blessings they received. Thanks, Dad, for your blessings of faithfulness, generosity, godliness, and family unity. Only a few families enjoy parental blessings in the ways we are.

> *From the burial instructions he left and the many little notes of encouragement that we found in his study after his death, we can say that Dad left us a great legacy of blessings.*

Shakespeare, speaking through Mark Anthony, offers the often-quoted words: "The evil that men do lives after them, the good is oft interred with their bones." Such words might be right in the world where humanity likes to recite the bad things about people, even though, at funerals and memorials, people say some of the nicest things, though, in whispers, some people seek to recall the worst about the dead. Yet, in the frame of the biblical patriarchs, matriarchs, and godly men and women of multiple generations, there is a difference. While their faults and failures might be whispered, their good deeds are recorded in what the Bible calls, "the book of remembrance." The prophet Malachi speaks of remembering the good deeds of those who breathed their last as follows:

" 'So now we call the proud blessed, for those who do wickedness are raised up; They even tempt God and go free.' Then those who feared the LORD spoke to one another, And the LORD listened and heard them; so a book of remembrance was written before Him for those who fear the Lord and who meditate on His name." (Mal. 3:15, 16, NKJV)

What is written in this book of remembrance? I cannot tell for sure, but I suspect that God takes note of the blessings the faithful have left for all those they encountered in this life. Yes, I do not know for sure, but I suspect that what is written are such things as:

1. The sweet influences that have been cast upon others
2. The kind words that have been spoken to others
3. The positive versus the adverse actions that have been done to others
4. The love that has been shared with others
5. The unpretentious friendships that have been shared with others
6. The songs that have been planted in the hearts of others
7. The generous, gracious gifts that have been given to others
8. The altars that have been built in families to the worship of God
9. The wells that have been dug to quench the thirst of others
10. The books that have been written or shared to bless the minds of others
11. The healing that has been brought to broken hearts
12. The poetry of life that have been passed on to soothe the hearts of others
13. The flowers that have been brought to others
14. The sacrifices and investments that have been made for the help or salvation of others
15. The "will" left to bless others.

There are multiple ways in which we can bring blessings to others, and these blessings do not end with our death but are shared with generations beyond. Here is what Julian Morgenstern states in his 1920 commentary in reflecting on Sarah, Abraham, and Jacob's death in the book of Genesis:

> And when our time comes to go hence and stand at last in the presence of our Maker, may we go like Sarah and Abraham and Jacob and all the patriarchs of old, leaving behind us some to mourn for us and to weep, and a memory which shall be for a blessing unto

those who come after us. Then we shall not have lived in vain, but shall have realized the purpose for which God placed us here on earth and gave us life; then through us will all the families of the earth be blessed (Julian Morgenstern, A Jewish Interpretation of the Book of Genesis).

The Christian songwriter, Jon Mohr, captures the essence of the comment on such blessings of life in his 1987 song:

We're pilgrims on the journey of the narrow road,
and those who've gone before us line the way,
cheering on the faithful, encouraging the weary,
their lives a stirring testament to God's sustaining grace.

Surrounded by so great a cloud of witnesses,
let us run the race not only for the prize,
but as those who've gone before us,
let us leave to those behind us,
the heritage of faithfulness passed on through godly lives.

Oh, may all who come behind us find us faithful,
May the fire of our devotion light their way,
May the footprints that we leave lead them to believe,
And the lives we live inspire them to obey,
Oh, may all who come behind us find us faithful.

After all our hopes and dreams have come and gone, and our children sift through all we've left behind, May the clues that they discover and the memories they uncover become the light that leads them to the road we each must find. ("Find Us Faithful")

Jon Mohr confesses to having written these words when he was just returning from a life in the "wild." He shared the words with his friend, the Christian singer and songwriter, Steve Green, who kept appealing to him. For a time, Mohr was so deep in "sinful lust" (his words) that he could not see how to get out. His heart was troubled. But one day, as the Spirit of God spoke to him, he yielded, and his life took the turn of which he writes.

In effect, maybe you have not been one of the most faithful parents. Perhaps you have made a mess of life and now wish that you can leave more positive blessings in your trail. Here is my reminder to you—that God can help you to do better. God can bless you even now with your last breath; you can be a blessing.

Take a Moment

Write down the blessing that the above reading has brought to your mind today and for which you would wish to thank the Lord.

_____
_____
_____
_____
_____
_____

Further, write down a special blessing that you would wish to ask the Lord to give you.

_____
_____
_____
_____
_____
_____

Then, write down how and with whom you would wish to share your blessing.

_____
_____
_____
_____
_____
_____

46.

Blessing the Lord

In concluding this book on the legacy of blessings from the book of Genesis, I turn to an issue that has been of interest, throughout the reflections, namely the phrase, "Blessed be the LORD." The phrase was first stated by Noah, when he awoke from his drunkenness and declared blessings on two of his sons, namely Shem and Japheth, and then pronounced a curse on his grandson Canaan, the son of Ham (Gen. 9:24–27). The phrase was then recited by Melchizedek, as he celebrated with Abraham as he was returning from battle against Amraphael king of Shinar, Chedorlaomer of Elam, and their cohort of kings (Gen. 14:20). And then the phrase was repeated by Eliezer of Damascus, the servant of Abraham, after he completed his successful mission to find a wife for Isaac, the heir of Abraham (Gen. 24:27, 48).

Without giving further details on the contexts of the phrase in each case, it is of interest to note that this is a most significant phrase. I have noted that many commentators give great attention to the blessing that comes from God and passed to other human beings, but they miss the blessing that humans give to God. So, I wish to make the point that, even before we share blessings given to us with others, we are to give our blessings back to God. The three stories I cited above illustrate that the blessings received come from God are first to be given back to God and then are to be shared with others. David said it this way: "Everything comes from you, and we have given you only what comes from your hand" (1 Chron. 29:14, NIV). Yes, following are the reasons that the blessing of God is repeated in the Genesis accounts:

- God is worthy to be blessed.
- He is the Creator of all.
- He is Sovereign over all.
- He is the source of all.
- He is faithful to all.

> *Even before we share blessings given to us with others, we are to give our blessings back to God.*

Yes, the most effective response that we can offer to the Lord for the copious blessings that He gives to us are blessings returned to the Lord. Psalm 103 is a model. Read it if you will. I have only included verses 1, 2, 20, 21, 22 as they are rendered in the KJV:

- Bless the LORD, O my soul: and all that is within me, bless his holy name.
- Bless the LORD, O my soul, and forget not all his benefits:
- Bless the LORD, ye his angels, that excel in strength, that do his commandments, hearkening unto the voice of his word.
- Bless ye the LORD, all ye his hosts; ye ministers of his, that do his pleasure.
- Bless the LORD, all his works in all places of his dominion: bless the Lord, O my soul.

This is not empty blessings or praise, as some individuals like to offer in engaging in worship. No, the motivation is as is stated in many parts of Scripture and framed in Psalm 116:

- What shall I return to the LORD for all his goodness to me?

And the answer is:

- I will lift up the cup of salvation and call on the name of the LORD.
- I will fulfill my vows to the LORD in the presence of all his people
- I will sacrifice a thank offering to you and call on the name of the LORD.
- I will fulfill my vows to the Lord in the presence of all his people … Praise the LORD. (Ps. 116:12–14, 17–19, NIV)

We have been told that there are many souls who wrestle for special victories and special blessings that they may do some great thing. However, having received the blessings they forget to "flip" the blessings in blessing the Lord and in blessing others.

While trying to count the multiple blessings that I have received in my life, I could not count them all. Nonetheless, I wish to share 101 that I have written down. The older I get, the more I am blessing God for His blessings.

1. The capacity to smell
2. The joy of eating
3. The ability to walk
4. The power to sit up
5. The strength to stand
6. The capacity to reason
7. The ability to speak
8. The capacity for relationship
9. Having a sound mind
10. The capacity for the bathroom
11. Putting on my clothes
12. The ability to see
13. Feeding myself
14. Breathing
15. The circulation of my blood
16. Visionariness
17. Forgiveness
18. The greenery of the earth
19. Good books to read
20. The privilege of prayer
21. Decision making
22. The freedom to choose
23. Self-control
24. Good weather
25. Traveling
26. Memory
27. Singing
28. Drawing
29. Strength
30. Beauty
31. Seeing
32. Laughing
33. Hearing
34. Feeling
35. Touching
36. Drinking
37. Mentors and mentees

38. Sharing
39. Peace
40. Protection
41. Provision
42. Presence
43. Preservation
44. Commandments
45. Preservation of life
46. Kindness
47. Supporting
48. Healing
49. Loving
50. The support of the community
51. Crying
52. Marriage
53. Star-gazing nights
54. Imagination
55. Interpretation
56. The beauty of nature
57. Sunshine
58. The Bible as the word
59. Salvation
60. Rain
61. Sunshine
62. Rain
63. Snow
64. The seasons
65. Grace
66. Mercy
67. Music
68. Hospitality
69. Logical thinking
70. Discerning the truth
71. Family
72. Communication
73. Creativity
74. My church community
75. Good friends

76. My parents
77. Our children
78. My spouse
79. My nieces and nephews
80. My siblings
81. Health and healing
82. Waking up each day
83. A heart that beats
84. Money to spend
85. Great teachers
86. My education
87. Where I was born
88. Clean water
89. A comfortable bed
90. Encouraging people
91. Quiet time for personal development
92. Electricity
93. Diversity
94. Rain and the rainbow
95. The ability to write
96. The ability to exercise
97. Adversity
98. A curious mind
99. The gift of songs
100. The gift of worship
101. Keeping the curses of life away

Yes, I bless the Lord for all the good gifts He has given me. They are too numerous to mention. I can only say with the Psalmist:

> I will praise You, for I am fearfully and wonderfully made; marvelous are Your works, and that my soul knows very well. (Ps. 139:14, NKJV)

I bless God most for who He is in all His perfections. He is to be thanked and greatly to be praised. Like the Psalmist says once again:

> I will bless the LORD at all times; His praise shall continually be in my mouth. (Ps. 34:1, NKJV)

I bless the Lord, not only for what I receive but for the blessings that I can share. The apostle Paul wrote:

> God can pour on the blessings in astonishing ways so that you're ready for anything and everything, more than just ready to do what needs to be done. (2 Cor. 9:8, MSG)

The list above are my big take always from my reflection on the legacy of blessings in Genesis. God blesses me; I bless the Lord, and I seek to bless everything about me—not only among those who are contemporaneous with me but all who will come behind me.

If you like what you have read in *A Legacy of Blessings*, connect with me for other books in the Legacy Series and for speaking appointments, seminars, and workshops in family life education and mentorship.

Legacy Seminars LLC
website: thelegacyseminars.com
Email: legacyseminars41@gmail.com
Phone: 862-224-1097
11503 Belvidere Road
Bowie, MD 20721

Reflections on A Legacy of Blessings

When I think of a legacy of blessings, it comes to me that most dominant among my siblings and I is our capacity to work creatively, diligently, and excellently in whatever we do. These qualities were carefully instilled in us by our parents who would never allow us to short-end anything. My effort to instill these qualities in the three sons that God has given to my husband and me has proven to be a legacy of blessing as I see it being generated in our grandchildren. I join my husband in praying that the legacy will be replicated in succeeding generations to the glory of God.

—S. June E. Kennedy, Ed. D, Relationship Coach, Family Life Educator Retired Public School, College Educator

When I think of *A Legacy of Blessings*, within my family, what I have heard from my earliest years is, "You have to control your destiny, you don't wait for other people to tell you how things need to happen—what to do and where to go."

My grandparents on both sides shared the idea that we needed to lead and not follow. They believed in the value of hard work but not just for the sake of working—they believed that the purpose of one's work is to contribute to a better life for others, especially those you love. And we couldn't wait until others handed us opportunities.

Now, with my own children, our encouragement to them is "do your best, operate with excellence and go for the highest you can in every opportunity. Don't wait until others go first. Step out and go for what you believe in."

—Robert D. Kennedy, III, M. Ed., President of Kennetik Kommunications

It's been interesting over the years to see what kind of genetic and nurtured "hand-me-downs" I've received from my parents and to see if it made it to my children. So, the easy go to would be leadership because it seems to flow through both sides of my family, and I just watch my children not being able help themselves in getting into leadership. The legacy that I tend to dwell on often is the creative legacy space. It tends to come across in music and artistic things, but I notice it with my children in their writings, their cooking and baking, and with so many other areas. It's nice to see the good things that get passed on.

—Leighton Kennedy, CRNP-PMH, PMHNP-BC
Clinical Director/Psychiatric Nursing Practitioner
Innova Life LLC: Behavioral Health Practice

When I look at the history of our family, I see a history of longevity—longevity in living, longevity in learning. But the thing I picked up was the longevity in loving. It is a biblical principal that I see in everything that my parents and grandparents did: LOVE each other. And I try to show my children love. Love is not always smiling, but it always has a purpose. To paraphrase a text: For God so LOVED the world that He gave His only Son that whosoever believes in Him won't perish but have eternal life. For God to give up His only son was not easy. It HURT! But it had a purpose! So back to the legacy of love—I will teach my boys to love with purpose.

—Sheldon Kennedy, BA, Producer,
Kennetick Koncepts, LLC

As I reflect on Dr. D. Robert Kennedy's *A Legacy of Blessings*, I become more conscious of my family's legacy through four generations. I see the striving for excellence, which drove my father and mother, my brother and me, then my two daughters, and it is now being clearly manifested in my four grandchildren. The meticulous pursuit of the spiritual and practical life has given me pause to say that it is a generational thing. Every person needs to script legacy blessings that they would wish to share through succeeding generations.

—Patrice Douglas, MA, MS High School English Teacher, New York City Board of Education

TEACH Services, Inc.
P U B L I S H I N G

We invite you to view the complete
selection of titles we publish at:
www.TEACHServices.com

We encourage you to write us
with your thoughts about this,
or any other book we publish at:
info@TEACHServices.com

TEACH Services' titles may be purchased in
bulk quantities for educational, fund-raising,
business, or promotional use.
bulksales@TEACHServices.com

Finally, if you are interested in seeing
your own book in print, please contact us at:
publishing@TEACHServices.com

We are happy to review your manuscript at no charge.

www.ingramcontent.com/pod-product-compliance
Lightning Source LLC
Chambersburg PA
CBHW071145160426
43196CB00011B/2015